# Character

# and Characterization

# in Shakespeare

*by*

Leo Kirschbaum

PROFESSOR OF ENGLISH
WAYNE STATE UNIVERSITY

Detroit    Wayne State University Press    1962

*To*
*M. A. Shaaber*

# *Preface*

*T*he essays in this volume deal with one facet of my
interest in Shakespeare in the past two decades. I have been
concerned with some puzzling persons in his plays, and not
being satisfied with what the critics by and large have said
about them, I have attempted to reanalyze and reinterpret
them afresh, remembering especially that they are characters
in a play with particular dramatic functions.

Five of the essays have been previously published, and
they are reprinted here as they originally appeared except for
minor revisions necessary to make them consistent with the
demands of a single publication. My thanks are due to the
editors of the following periodicals for permission to reprint
these five:

*Shakespeare Association Bulletin* (now *Shakespeare Quar-
terly*), XIX (1944), 161-71, for "Shakespeare's Cleopatra";
*English Literary History,* published by The Johns Hopkins
Press, XI (1944), 283-96, for "The Modern Othello";

*Philological Quarterly,* XXXV (1956), 325-93, for "Hamlet and Ophelia";

*Essays in Criticism,* VII (1957), 1-21, for "Banquo and Edgar: Character or Function?";

*Shakespeare Survey 13,* published by Cambridge University Press (1960), pp. 20-29, for "Albany."

My numbering and readings, unless otherwise noted, come from Peter Alexander, editor, *William Shakespeare, The Complete Works* (London and Glasgow, 1951).

L. K.

# Contents

*Character
and Characterization
in Shakespeare*

# Introduction

After so much excellent work undermining the critical assumptions of A. C. Bradley's *Shakespearean Tragedy*—which, because of Bradley's fine insights, often antithetic to his general "realistic" approach to character and plot, is not quite the simple target most of the *avant garde* Shakespeare critics take it to be—it should be a dictum today that Shakespeare wrote a *poetic* drama and not an Ibsenian one. But it is not. The greatest danger to an appreciation of Shakespeare is still the inveterate, unswervable naturalistic-psychological approach. I find it, blatantly on the surface or hidden below it, even in the writing of sophisticated modern critics. I perceive its menace in my students at every class meeting.

As an emphasizer of the tenet that Shakespeare did not write naturalistic drama, however, I must also emphasize that I am not a fellow of those moderns who see in his individual plays only themes (e.g., L. C. Knights), or images (e.g., R. B. Heilman), or progressive spiritual development (e.g., D. A.

1

Traversi). In their revolt against the so-called "romantic" school, which often emphasized character to the exclusion of everything else, many contemporary critics have gone so far in the other direction that their conclusions, too, seem partial and esoteric. They, too, have fastened on parts to the exclusion of the whole. To me Shakespeare wrote plays for a theatre, and his theatrical success is ultimately the center of all my interest. I refuse to denigrate in the least—for the benefit of the so-called higher accoutrements: theme, image, or thought —the old-fashioned major attraction of plot, however recondite I may become in allying plot with overall design, in which the poetry, the image, the thought, and particularly the architecture of passage, scene, and act play their part. Furthermore, I am as intensely interested in Shakespeare's characters as any misguided nineteenth century bardolater. But I want to know how within the acknowledged territory of poetic drama Shakespeare handled problems of character and characterization. Briefly, *character* refers to what one of the *dramatis personae* is or becomes psychologically and ethically: *characterization,* to the method or methods by which the author sets forth that personage.

Outside the pioneer efforts of E. E. Stoll, which deserve separate treatment, and will receive it in a moment, the problem of character in Shakespeare has, queerly enough, not received much attention in this century. L. L. Schücking in his *Character Problems in Shakespeare's Plays* (1922) was also a pioneer: but criticizing obviously, not to say ostentatiously, from the viewpoint of realistic drama, he could only, pejoratively and irritatingly, dwell on Shakespeare's "primitive" technique; could only see his characterization, despite temporary aberrations, as "essentially realistic" (p. 179); and failed constantly in particular analyses to be sensitive to *all* the im-

2

plications of the poetic situation. S. L. Bethell in *Shakespeare and the Popular Dramatic Tradition* (1944) was much more careful, stressing—correctly, I believe—that Shakespeare's characterization was founded on the methodology of earlier English drama and was therefore a mixed mode of the conventional and the realistic, at one time this, at another that, at times both. In this approach he was seconded by W. B. C. Watkins' *Shakespeare and Spenser* (1950), which again indicates that the mixed mode which Shakespeare employs is one of psychological realism *and* the symbolical. Probably the very best critical statement of the role of character in Shakespeare's drama has been made by the acute Henri Fluchère in his *Shakespeare* (1953): the "author's dramatic purpose" must be the all-compelling motive in the analysis of any character; characterization is merely one part of the whole and must bow to the needs of the whole (p. 137). Nevertheless, Fluchère does not often—for lack of space, I suppose—come to immediate grips with the particular problems of character and characterization in the individual plays he treats. His views on such problems, while enlightening, are fragmentary within the embracing critique.

How can one be fair today to E. E. Stoll? Since its heyday in the thirties, his influence has, I believe, steadily waned. Only eleven years after Bradley's opus, Stoll, in *Othello* (1915), had already begun his great attack against the nineteenth century's romantic approach to Shakespeare. His culminating effort was *Art and Artifice in Shakespeare* (1933). The ordinary reader, apart from the scholar, who wants to get the Stoll view *in toto* without too much search, should look at his *From Shakespeare to Joyce* (1944).

Basically, I believe, what is wrong with Stoll is that he cannot admit the charismatic effect of art—that, when all is

3

said and done, art is mysterious in creation and in effect. He is a rationalist who is violently disturbed by any attribution of higher powers to the poet, by the implicit assertion that the audience *felt* correctly rather than *reasoned* correctly. The "psychology" he employs for his character analyses is often extremely naive. If he had only understood, as St. Augustine, Calvin, and Freud understood, the complete inexplicability on rational terms of the drive toward evil in the human heart! If, only, he had understood the refusal on occasion of the great artist to do more than *suggest!* If, only, like Longinus and Coleridge, he had been more often willing to admit literary grandeur!

Ultimately, I think, Stoll did not understand poetic drama, and was both attracted and repelled by the poetic techniques of Shakespeare. Still, our debt to him is immense. He taught us principles, even if we have to be leery of his own applications of them. He constantly pointed out the unrealism of Shakespeare's plays, the constant use of theatrical conventions, the frequent non-psychological motivations, the frequent use of type or stock characters, and the analogies with past or contemporary non-realistic drama (e.g., of Molière). My own debt to him is very great.

It remains to give a summary of the contents of the present book. I do not mind being accused of inconsistency. What applies to *Much Ado* is not necessarily what applies to *Othello*. Shakespeare was an inveterate experimenter, and his plays refuse to be pigeon-holed. Nevertheless, it probably remains generally true that the production of a Shakespeare play should more resemble one of Aeschylus' than one of Lee Strassberg and Elia Kazan's, followers of Stanislavsky.

Each essay in the book tries to deal with a particular problem of character and characterization in a particular play. The

4

sum of the observations may illustrate how multiple Shakespeare's ways of fitting the character or characters to a play were. The essay on *The Merchant of Venice* shows the embellishment of a traditional stage villain and the submergence of the individual "good" character within group characteristics; that on *King Lear*, the immense character development in one of the dramatic personages, Albany, whose growth is essential to the total significance of the play; that on *Macbeth* and *King Lear*, dealing with Banquo and Edgar, the utilization of character for dramatically functional purposes, psychology being more or less abrogated; that on *Hamlet*, the difficulty apparently intended by the dramatist in interpreting the relationship between two of the major characters, Hamlet and Ophelia; that on *Antony and Cleopatra*, the unity of a dazzling character, Cleopatra, gained by the poetic employment of a related group of images; that on *Romeo and Juliet*, the shift of a character, Romeo, from convention to a romantic kind of realism by means of a change in style; that on *Measure for Measure*, the psychological bifurcation of an essential character, Angelo; that on *Much Ado About Nothing*, the divergence between melodramatic and realistic characterization and character; that on *Richard II*, the establishment of character by "blocking"; and that on *Othello*, the possibility of psychological interpretation of a character, the Moor, whom many critics consider the creation merely of conventions.

There are three further points: (1) My emphasis on Shakespeare's artifice is meant in no way to detract from the individual play's theatrical success. That Angelo and Margaret are divided characterizations does not at all mean that I consider them, as they function within the whole, theatrical failures. On the contrary, as I see it, my task has been to reveal the poet's legerdemain—an understanding of which may give

5

further pleasure to certain minds which want to know how they have been "fooled," to put it platonically. (2) That the bifurcation of Angelo and Margaret occurs because of report of their activities rather through their own speeches and actions on the boards is certainly a part of Shakespeare's planning, but this does not mean that *in the theatre* appearance is to be considered more trustworthy than honest report. The character is no more "real" when he is before us than when he is away from us. To deny this is to confuse life and art. That there is more dramatic emphasis on direct presentation than on indirect trustworthy report or *vice versa* is another critical problem altogether, which probably does concern our ultimate reactions to Angelo. That the two Margarets are equally emphasized, that the one reported is stressed as much as the one appearing, is part of the fun of *Much Ado*. (3) Finally— and I tend to repeat myself somewhat—I do not want the reader to think that I am supplying him with an invaluable vade mecum that will solve every character problem in Shakespeare. I offer no such general program, even by implication. Each Shakespeare play requires its own special treatment. Each character in each play deserves separate examination. New categories of character may have to be found, new methods of characterization may have to be investigated.

What must be stressed, however, is the folly of automatically adhering willy-nilly to the *a priori* "romantic" notion that every Shakespeare character is as real in unity, depth, and complexity as the reader of this book.

# 1

# Shylock in the City of God

*The Merchant of Venice* is a fantasy—but it is, at bottom, a serious fantasy. Its characters are not deeply drawn; its plot is providential; its atmosphere is unrealistic—but the conflict of values it illustrates was important to Shakespeare's own time. Difficult as it may be, let us suspend our own values, our contemporary basic decencies, if you wish, and strive to become members of a 1596 audience. Let us, in short, see what Shakespeare meant by *Jew* and *Christian* in his play so that we may come to understand a fifth act which is a triumph of moonlight, music, friendship, love, and laughter—a fifth act which so many people today must regard as extraneous and, perhaps, nasty after the fall of poor, persecuted Shylock.

There were no Jewish communities in England in Shakespeare's time. The rare individuals of Hebraic origin that history discovers in sixteenth century England merely enforce the point. Theatergoers could no more encounter kinsmen of

Shylock in the streets of London than they could encounter kinsmen of Caliban. To the playwright and his auditors, Jews were almost as mythical as anthropophagi. Shakespeare's source for Shylock was not life but literature and folklore. In them the Jew was typed as an anti-Christian, usurious, cruel monster. This is the stereotyped figure which Shakespeare utilized for Shylock. And these are the traits which his spectators would expect in any stage Jew. Shylock would immediately be recognized as alien to the City of God, the ideal Christian community of the Middle Ages—and of the Reformation too, as Zurich and Geneva witness. But Shakespeare put the folklore Jew to new purposes. He infused the pasteboard figure with a range of attitudes and traits which symbolize the vast disruptive forces of sixteenth century Europe. The Christian community of Venice—i.e., the City of God—which Shylock threatens is an idealized projection of a real England which felt and saw but could not completely understand what was undermining it. As scapegoat, Shakespeare's Jew would provide a London audience of the 1590's with a satisfying release of resentments and frustrations, a kind of catharsis.

In Shakespeare's time the past was breaking up. Tradition and actuality were at variance. In the City of God communal values had always superseded private ones. But in the sixteenth century there was abroad a *new* idea, so disturbing that it became a bugaboo to frighten grown-ups, the idea of ruthless and iconoclastic individualism, as epitomized by the real and the pseudo-Machiavelli and by the doctrine of *virtù*, the uninhibited exploitation of all one's innate abilities and powers. Concomitantly, in the economic realm, commerce and industry were beginning to displace agriculture as the most expedient means to wealth. The discovery of the Americas showered

8

Europe with riches that had been neither toiled nor spun for. The force of events was creating Economic Man—but not, as yet, his justification. In short, our modern financial era of commerce and industry was beginning. Furthermore, the Reformation was fracturing the European community, by state and within state, into antagonistic pluralities. A pervasive fear of *otherness* began to grow. English nationalism rose to a high tide; but in England itself, Catholic, Anglican, and Puritan feared and hated one another. So Shakespeare set before his definitely Anglican, definitely patriotic, and definitely conservative audience a monster, Shylock, in whom disruptive individualism, economic aggrandizement, and perturbing uncanniness appear at their most frightening and melodramatic.

Marlowe had showed Shakespeare the way. A few years before *The Merchant of Venice,* the former had brilliantly indicated what could be done with the folklore Jew to exploit the fears and resentments of Elizabethan London. In the prologue of *The Jew of Malta,* Machiavelli describes to the spectators his follower, Barrabas. The Jew's real God in the play is not Jehovah, but gold, won not by labor but by usury and sea commerce. Reviling the Christians and their values, he has no loyalties to anyone but himself—not to his synagogue, not to his daughter. He is anarchic in his desires for power and wealth—hypocritical, cunning, and murderous. Nevertheless, Marlowe's Jew and the other inhabitants of his play lack the immediacy of Shakespeare's figures. Barrabas is a competitor rather than an antagonist of the Christians, and the latter are by no means so differentiated from him that an English audience would automatically care to identify itself with them.

Shylock is more acclimatized to England than Barrabas. Shakespeare has given Shylock certain traits that tie him closely to the actuality of the times. He has much of the popular

9

concept of the Puritan in him. Shylock is sober, industrious, Bible-quoting, hypocritical, assertive, and ruthless—and he is ostentatiously a kill-joy. He is a projection of the hatred the more easy-going Anglicans felt for the righteous sectists, whom obscurely they were beginning to associate with economic aggressiveness and cupidity.[1] Again, Shakespeare emphasizes very much Shylock's apartness from the Christian community. It is stressed again and again that he is not a citizen of Venice, that he is an *alien,* a *foreigner,* a *stranger.* The ordinary London citizen violently disliked the foreign craftsmen from Flanders, Germany, and France (known as *aliens, strangers, foreigners*) who were allowed by special governmental dispensation to live and work in London. All through the sixteenth century there were resentment, agitation, and sometimes riots against them. Ill-feeling was especially strong in 1595.

Shylock, then, is not an imitation of a real Jew. He is meant to symbolize those antisocial traits which conventional society felt were inimical to their traditional sense of the normal and the decent. The Christian community in the play is meant to symbolize the preservation of these traditional values even in an era of economic expansion. Hence, in one way, Shylock *is* more real than the Christians in the drama, for he after all does derive from reality. The Elizabethans could not meet Jews, but they could meet Englishmen who, they thought, by and large, stood for what Shylock stood for. The play's Christian characters and their destiny, on the other hand, are a wish-fulfillment, a vision of goodness dreamt in the reality of an increasingly acquisitive society.

Let us examine the Christian values of the play. (As a matter of fact, most of the Christian characters are more depictions of values than they are attempts at giving the illusion of substantial dimensionality. To seek psychological depth in them is not only aesthetically wrong but dramatically destructive: they are meant to be felt as the not too differentiated and discrete cells of a single organism, the Christian community.) Since it bulks so large in the play, let us begin with the subject of money. When he looks at the three caskets, Bassanio says,

> Therefore, thou gaudy gold,
> Hard food for Midas, I will none of thee;
> Nor none of thee, thou pale and common drudge
> 'Tween man and man.

Since gold is not edible, it actually represents a kind of starvation unless used properly; silver, disreputable in itself, is a necessary slave that administers to men's requirements. Wealth, therefore, should be but a means to an end, not an end in itself; hence thrift is not a virtue, and debt is not defilement. Bassanio at the beginning of the play admits to Antonio,

> 'Tis not unknown to you, Antonio,
> How much I have disabled mine estate
> By something showing a more swelling port
> Than my faint means would grant continuance.

Antonio does not blame him at all. Let me know your plan, he says,

> And if it stand, as you yourself still do,
> Within the eye of honor, be assur'd
> My purse, my person, my extremest means
> Lie all unlock'd to your occasions.

Money, it is indicated, should be treated with a certain contempt, as in Portia's lines,

> Pay him six thousand, and deface the bond.
> Double six thousand and then treble that
> Before a friend of this description
> Shall lose a hair through Bassanio's fault.

11

Or in her refusal of ducats, when she is in disguise,

> He is well paid that is well satisfied,
> And I, delivering you, am satisfied,
> And therein do account myself well paid.
> My mind was never yet more mercenary.

Obviously, to the Christians in the play, money is a good only in so far as it serves human needs; and these needs are indirectly expressed by Portia when she speaks of "companions/That do converse and waste the time together." In other words, at the banquet of life, in innocent, pleasant, and cultured amity, sit a group of friends.

From the start of the play, the ease of such a fellowship is defined. It consists of laughter, dining, beauty, entertainment, music, conversation, gifts, and similar graces of humane society. Sometimes, this social ease takes the form of appropriate ritual: Bassanio tells Antonio that he needs "the means/To hold a rival place" with Portia's other suitors. Sometimes, this social ease takes the form of carefree expenditure: Lorenzo and Jessica spend money freely on their honeymoon in gambling and silly purchases. When they return, they are more or less penniless—but, significantly, Portia leaves "The husbandry and manage of my house" to Lorenzo. Always, if possible, in this Christian society, there should be innocent pleasure. Bassanio, for example, must have a "supper" before he leaves for Belmont. It is to be a merry occasion. Gratiano is not to try to be demure at it. Bassanio declares,

> I would entreat you rather to put on
> Your boldest suit of mirth, for we have friends
> That purpose merriment.

Gratiano, Lorenzo, Salerio, and Salanio are preparing a surprise entertainment for the occasion. There will be masks,

12

disguises, and torchbearers; and the masquers will be pre-
ceded by music, the drum and the fife. Music is important to
these people. It plays while Bassanio chooses among the
caskets. And music and the music of the spheres, those symbols
of harmony, play a large part in the Lorenzo-Jessica overture
to the love and friendship paean of the last act:

> The man that hath no music in himself,
> Nor is not mov'd with concord of sweet sounds,
> Is fit for treasons, stratagems, and spoils;
> The motions of his spirit are dull as night,
> And his affections dark as Erebus.
> Let no such man be trusted. Mark the music.

But theirs is definitely not a hedonistic existence. Pleasure
is not their chief good; it is an ancillary good. It is not so
much that their religion is urbane as that their urbanity is
religious. Human beings, they believe, are distinguished from
animals by a natural tendency toward good and by reason.
The Duke says that Antonio's bad luck would receive pity
"From stubborn Turks and Tartars, never trained/To offices
of tender courtesy." When Shylock refuses to give a "firm
reason" why he is being so brutal to Antonio except a non-
rational "certain loathing," Bassanio breaks out, "This is no
answer, thou unfeeling man." A man who acts without reason
or charity is like an animal; therefore, Gratiano cries at
Shylock,

> Thou almost mak'st me waver in my faith,
> To hold opinion with Pythagoras,
> That souls of animals infuse themselves
> Into the trunks of men.

The Christians in the play are well aware of the religious
facts of life and death: original sin, redemption, baptism,

prayer, grace, damnation, and salvation. Portia links Christian eschatology and the Lord's Prayer:

> Though justice be thy plea, consider this—
> That, in the course of justice, none of us
> Should see salvation. We do pray for mercy,
> And that same prayer doth teach us all to render
> The deeds of mercy.

"The course of justice" refers not merely to the individual but to mankind. She is referring to redemption from the just damnation of man by the mercy of the Christ. The prime purpose of life is salvation:

> It is very meet
> The Lord Bassanio live an upright life;
> For, having such a blessing in his lady,
> He finds the joys of heaven here on earth;
> And if on earth he do not merit it,
> In reason he should never come to heaven.

Lorenzo, in speaking of the music of the spheres, refers to immortality and its place in the order of the universe:

> Such harmony is in immortal souls;
> But whilst this muddy vesture of decay
> Doth grossly close it in, we cannot hear it.

A Christian can laugh at religious hypocrisy which emphasizes the outward for the sake of social approval:

> If I do not put on a sober habit,
> Talk with respect, and swear but now and then,
> Wear prayer books in my pocket, look demurely,
> Nay more, while grace is saying, hood mine eyes
> Thus with my hat, and sigh, and say amen,
> Use all the observance of civility
> Like one well studied in a sad ostent
> To please his grandam, never trust me more.

14

But heresy is a serious matter and must be hated:

> The devil can cite Scripture for his purpose.
> An evil soul, producing holy witness,
> Is like a villain with a smiling cheek.

>                           In religion,
> What damned error but some sober brow
> Will bless it, and approve it with a text,
> Hiding the grossness with fair ornament.

The religion of the Christian characters is reverent but not
ostentatious. We hear that Portia, returning to Belmont,

>                    doth stray about
> By holy crosses, where she kneels and prays
> For happy wedlock hours.

She is accompanied, it is said, by "a holy hermit," who may
or may not be part of the white lie she has told Lorenzo and
Jessica:

> I have toward heaven breath'd a secret vow
> To live in prayer and contemplation
> Only attended by Nerissa here,
> Until her husband and my lord's return.
> There is a monastery two miles off,
> And there we will abide.

Coupled with the contempt in the play for money as money
is the Christian principle that one must trust to Providence
more than to mortal prudence. (Tawney suggests that the
core of the ecclesiastical hatred of usury was the certainty of
gain, the lack of risk on the part of the lender.—*Religion and
the Rise of Capitalism*, Pelican Books, p. 44.) The true Christian view is finely expressed in Launcelot Gobbo's words to
Bassanio:

15

*Launcelot:* The old proverb is very well parted between my
master Shylock and you, sir. You have the grace of God,
sir, and he hath enough.
*Bassanio:* Thou speak'st it well.

He that has the grace of God has enough; God will take care
of his own. And this is implicit in what Nerissa tells Portia
concerning the caskets:

> Your father was ever virtuous; and holy men at their
> death have good inspirations. Therefore the lott'ry that
> he hath devised in these three chests of gold, silver, and
> lead, whereof who chooses his meaning chooses you, will
> no doubt never be chosen by any rightly but one who you
> shall rightly love.

Thus, to hazard is to have faith in Providence. Antonio tells
Shylock that Jacob's gain was due to Providence, not to human
device:

> This was a venture, sir, that Jacob serv'd for;
> A thing not in his power to bring to pass,
> But sway'd and fashion'd by the hand of heaven.

Antonio "ventures" his life to provide Bassanio with money.
And the right casket, the lead one, emphatically states the
principle of risk: "Who chooses me must give and hazard all
he hath." The word *hazard* runs through the play like a
refrain. Jessica and Lorenzo do not worry about the morrow,
but at the end of the play they are the inheritors of Shylock's
wealth.

That the Christian community is a spiritual organism is
postulated by the entire play. At the beginning of 3.4, Lorenzo
says to Portia, "You have a noble and a true conceit/Of godlike amity." This last phrase, *godlike amity,* adumbrates the
ideal view of society as the living body of Christ, as the City

16

of God: The all and the one are the same. Portia says to
Lorenzo,

> I never did repent for doing good,
> Nor shall not now; for in companions
> That do converse and waste the time together,
> Whose souls do bear an egal yoke of love,
> There must be needs a like proportion
> Of lineaments, of manners, and of spirit;
> Which makes me think that this Antonio,
> Being the bosom lover of my lord,
> Must needs be like my lord. If it be so,
> How little is the cost I have bestow'd
> In purchasing the semblance of my soul
> From out the state of hellish cruelty!
> This comes too near the praising of myself.
> Therefore no more of it.

In saving others one is saving oneself. In loving others properly
one is, in a theological sense, loving oneself properly. To be
virtuous to one another is to imitate God, to resemble God:
mercy, for example,

> is an attribute to God himself.
> And earthly power doth then show likest God's
> When mercy seasons justice.

Hence the marked expression of friendship in the play, hence
the emphatic assertion of the claims of charity.

Thus, the Christians in Shakespeare's Venice make up a
distinct society of Christian solicitude, each is concerned more
for others than for himself, all love Antonio. "Behind the
figure of Antonio," says Theodor Reik in *The Secret Self,* "is
the greater one of Jesus Christ." At the very beginning of the
play, Gratiano declares to Antonio: "I love thee, and it is my
love that speaks." A few lines later, Bassanio affirms similar

17

affection: "To you, Antonio, I owe the most, in money and in love." Salerio gives his opinion concerning their friend: "A kinder gentleman treads not the earth." Later Salanio talks of "the good Antonio, the honest Antonio—O that I had a title good enough to keep his name company!" Bassanio describes him to Portia:

> The dearest friend to me, the kindest man,
> The best-condition'd and unwearied spirit
> In doing courtesies.

Lorenzo also describes him,

> But if you knew to whom you show this honour,
> How true a gentleman you send relief,
> How dear a lover of my lord your husband,
> I know you would be prouder of the work
> Than customary bounty can enforce you.

Portia tells Bassanio to spend much money,

> Before a friend of this description
> Shall lose a hair through Bassanio's fault.

That all the Christians so admire and cherish Antonio is significant in relation to the values in the play. He represents the ideal standard of *caritas*. All true Christians are his friends, and he has saved many from Shylock's grasp. For the sake of Bassanio he is willing to give up not only his wealth but even life itself.

Race and color in themselves are not socially significant to these people. It is what a man or woman morally is and does that determines whether he or she should be accepted or not. Jessica, referring to her own concept of the good life, puts the matter succinctly: "But though I am a daughter to [my father's] blood,/I am not to his manners." Hence she adopts the faith the members of which do have the right

18

"manners." And she is completely accepted by these members. The treatment of Jessica by the Christians is testimony that within the circumscription of the play, Jews are hated not because of their "blood" but because of their "manners." Christian virtue can so translate the individual that racial distinctions disappear:

*Shylock:* I say my daughter is my flesh and blood.
*Salerio:* There is more difference between thy flesh and hers than between jet and ivory; more between your bloods than there is between red wine and Rhenish.

Hence, in all sincerity, when Antonio discovers that Shylock wants for the sake of "friendship" to charge him no interest, he says, "Hie thee, gentle Jew./The Hebrew will turn Christian; he grows kind." If by anti-Semitism is meant wholly irrational prejudice against Jews in general, it would be difficult to accuse any of the Christian characters in the play of that vice.

Let us now examine what Shakespeare means in the play by *Jew*. Observe Shylock at his first appearance in 1.3. Clad in his yellow gaberdine, he is visually the "stranger" within the gates, the "alien." He is not a citizen of the community, but a "foreigner." From the start, he is neither pathetic nor heroic but either sadistic or cringing.

*Shylock:* Antonio is a good man.
*Bassanio:* Have you heard any imputation to the contrary?
*Shylock:* Oh, no, no, no, no! My meaning in saying he is a good man is to have you understand me that he is sufficient.

Sufficient! Here is the essential doctrine of "economic man." *Good* has not merely shifted its meaning: it has shifted its

19

deity! Yet, Shylock goes on, Antonio has not been a careful businessman. His ships are over the many seas. "And other ventures he hath, squand'red abroad." In other words, Antonio has not been prudent; he has ventured, hazarded. But men cannot be trusted, declares the Jew. There are "land rats and water rats": thieves and pirates. Nor is nature beneficent. "There is the peril of waters, winds, and rocks." In such an inimical world of men and things, Shylock refuses to hazard. He will trust only his own judgment.

When Bassanio invites him to dinner to meet Antonio, Shylock gives his first example of twisting the Bible to his own uses: The swine into which Jesus sent the demons become the customary food of the Christians! Then Shylock follows with an extremely significant statement:

> I will buy with you, sell with you, talk with you,
> walk with you, and so following; but I will not
> eat with you, drink with you, nor pray with you.

Business is business. It has nothing to do with fellowship or religion. Here, then, is utter rejection of those Christian values which we have just analyzed. When Antonio enters, Shylock soliloquizes: "How like a fawning publican he looks." Shylock hates Antonio's self-abnegation, and Christian courtesy he interprets as fawning. Antonio has refused to be the economic man:

> I hate him for he is a Christian;
> But more for that in low simplicity
> He lends out money gratis and brings down
> The rate of usance here with us in Venice.

Note the "more." Shylock hates Antonio more for economic reasons than for racial or religious ones. Since cunning economic man gets all that he can get, Shylock ridicules Christian

20

charity as "low simplicity." Then, "If I can catch him once upon the hip,/I will feed fat the ancient grudge I bear him." Cannibalism in Shylock is already indicated.

> He hates our sacred nation, and he rails,
> Even there where merchants most do congregate,
> On me, my bargains, and my well-won thrift.

This is the first evidence of Shylock's ability to rationalize Christian hatred of his immorality into Christian hatred of his Jewishness. In other words, Shylock hypocritically covers up his own criminality by charging his accusers with anti-Semitism. In similar fashion, his usury becomes "bargains" and "well-won thrift."

To defend the malpractice of usury to Antonio, Shylock wracks Scripture in referring to the cunning Jacob and the pied lambs. But notice too another Biblical reference:

> This Jacob from our holy Abram was
> (As his wise mother wrought in his behalf)
> The third possessor.

The "wise mother" was Rebecca, who tricked the blind Isaac into blessing Jacob instead of Esau. Thus, the cunning of economic man becomes wisdom! And Shylock finishes his Biblical explication of Jacob with

> This was a way to thrive, and he was blest;
> And thrift is blessing, if men steal it not.

God blesses economic man, cunning is wisdom, and everything is justified except outright stealing! Will Shylock make the loan?

> Signior Antonio, many a time and oft
> In the Rialto you have rated me
> About my moneys and my usances.

21

> Still have I borne it with a patient shrug;
> For suff'rance is the badge of all our tribe.
> You call me misbeliever, cutthroat dog,
> And spit upon my Jewish gaberdine,
> And all for use of that which is mine own.

Antonio, it is clearly shown in this passage, hates Shylock because of his usury. But Shylock evades the issue: on the one hand, he says his Jewishness is the reason for this hatred; on the other hand, usury is not reprehensible: it is the "use of that which is mine own." Private judgment, Shylock implies, not communal judgment or welfare, should be the sole criterion in money matters.

Launcelot Gobbo is the "unthrifty knave" in whose risky care Shylock has left his house. We discover that he is so miserable as the Jew's servant that he wishes to run away. His master has not been giving him enough to eat: "I am famish'd in his service." Jessica in 2.3 indicates that we can trust the Clown's judgment: "Our house is hell; and thou, a merry devil,/Did'st rob it of some taste of tediousness." Why, from the Christian viewpoint, the house is hell is trenchantly suggested in 2.5. Shylock bullies his daughter and berates the unthrifty knave. Little food, little sleep, the frugalest necessities of clothing, constant labor for the master's prosperity—these are his theme. Launcelot hints that there will be a masque at the feast to which Shylock has been invited. Economic man is appalled at such epicureanism:

> What, are there masques? Hear you me, Jessica.
> Lock up my doors; and when you hear the drum
> And the vile squealing of the wry-neck'd fife,
> Clamber not you up to the casements then,
> Nor thrust your head into the public street
> To gaze on Christian fools with varnish'd faces;
> But stop my house's ears—I mean my casements.

22

> Let not the sound of shallow fopp'ry enter
> My sober house. By Jacob's staff I swear
> I have no mind of feasting forth tonight.

Neither his house nor its inhabitants are to hear the music or watch the procession. "Lock up my doors." A morris dance is as bad as stealing. "Stop my house's ears." Music destroys thrift. People who enjoy such vanities are "fools." His is a "sober house." And sobriety and cupidity suddenly coalesce in a reference to a Biblical personage who has already appeared as a symbol of business cunning, Jacob. Economic man in this scene is portrayed in all his unsleeping concern for frugality, rapid profit, and no leisure. In all his lack of human concern for his fellow man. And in all his aptness for proverbs of the Poor Richard type.

> The patch [Launcelot] is kind enough, but a huge feeder,
> Snail-slow in profit, and he sleeps by day
> More than the wildcat. Drones hive not with me. . . .

> Well, Jessica, go in.
> Perhaps I will return immediately.
> Do as I bid you; shut doors after you.
> Fast bind, fast find—
> A proverb never stale in thrifty mind.

We do not see Shylock again until 3.1. However, we learn of his reaction to his daughter's flight from Salanio in 2.8:

> "My daughter! O my ducats! O my daughter!
> Fled with a Christian! O my Christian ducats!
> Justice! the law! My ducats, and my daughter!
> A sealed bag, two sealed bags of ducats,
> Of double ducats, stolen from me by my daughter!
> And jewels—two stones, two rich and precious stones,
> Stol'n by my daughter! Justice! Find the girl!
> She hath the stones upon her, and the ducats!"

We may well agree with the Christian speaker that this is a strange and outrageous lament. It is not the loss of his child, nor even that she has been disloyal to him, which has sent Shylock into a passion. It is clearly the money and the jewels.

In 3.1 he rails at the bankrupt Antonio. Then comes one of Shylock's most famous—and most misunderstood!—declarations:

*Salerio:* Why, I am sure, if he forfeit, thou wilt not take his flesh. What's that good for?

*Shylock:* To bait fish withal. If it will feed nothing else, it will feed my revenge. He hath disgrac'd me, and hind'red me half a million; laugh'd at my losses, mock'd at my gains, scorned my nation, thwarted my bargains, cooled my friends, heated mine enemies—and what's his reason? I am a Jew. Hath not a Jew eyes? Hath not a Jew hands, organs, dimensions, senses, affections, passions? Fed with the same food, hurt with the same weapons, subject to the same diseases, healed by the same means, warmed and cooled by the same winter and summer as a Christian is? If you prick us, do we not bleed? If you tickle us, do we not laugh? If you poison us, do we not die? And if you wrong us, shall we not revenge? If we are like you in the rest, we will resemble you in that. If a Jew wrong a Christian, what is his humility? Revenge. If a Christian wrong a Jew, what should his sufferance be by Christian example? Why, revenge. The villainy you teach me I will execute, and it shall go hard but I will better the instruction.

Only eyes so blinded with sentimental tears that they cannot pierce hypocrisy, rationalization, and savagery can read this speech as a plausible justification of Shylock. He defends his cannibalism on grounds of revenge. Why? Antonio has hated him because he is a Jew. But the phrases before tell a different story. "Losses," "gains," "bargains," and "half a million" recall

24

the villainous business morality which Antonio has considered vile. The word is *ethic*, not *ethnic*, for Antonio's hatred. But Shylock wishes to make it *ethnic*. Is not a Jew a human being? The modern reader does not see here how completely Shylock is condemning himself. To be a human being means to act and feel as a human being. The more Shylock expounds on common physical attributes, the more definitely he is calling attention to the absence of common spiritual attributes. He claims that he has learned the principle of revenge from the Christians. But the "eye for an eye" Old Law has been replaced by the New Law, the Sermon on the Mount. And we shall see for ourselves later what Christian revenge is.

Shylock's egocentrism (his *real* concern for himself rather than his *exhibited* concern for his group), his placement of monetary loss skies higher than paternal loss, his fervid appetite for revenge even when it concerns his own flesh and blood—all these characteristics are brought out in his speech to Tubal:

> Why, there, there, there! A diamond gone cost me two thousand ducats in Frankford! The curse never fell upon our nation till now; I never felt it till now. Two thousand ducats in that, and other precious, precious jewels. I would my daughter were dead at my foot, and the jewels in her ear! Would she were hears'd at my foot, and the ducats in her coffin! No news of them? Why, so—and I know not what's spent in the search. Why, thou loss upon loss! the thief gone with so much, and so much to find the thief; and no satisfaction, no revenge! nor no ill luck stirring but what lights o' my shoulders; no sighs but o' my breathing; no tears but o' my shedding.

Mark Shylock's blasphemy when he is informed of Antonio's ill luck: "I thank God, I thank God! Is it true? is it true?" His gaiety is obscene. "Good news, good news! Ha, ha!" "I am very glad of it. I'll plague him, I'll torture him. I am glad of it." The critics are probably right in seeing real sentiment in his exclamation when told of the ring which Jessica sold for a monkey. "Out upon her! Thou torturest me, Tubal. It was my turquoise. I had it of Leah when I was a bachelor." But the same critics are sentimental in their treatment of this detail. Any touch that postulates humanity in Shylock blackens by contrast his inhumanity all the more. This is only one detail—the cannibalistic money-lender is revealed in his next words: "I will have the heart of [Antonio] if he forfeit; for, were he out of Venice, I can make what merchandise I will." Usury and murder are two sides of the same viciousness. And then Shakespeare presents a final nasty touch. After feeing an officer to arrest Antonio when his bond comes due, "good Tubal" is to meet Shylock "at our synagogue!"

Act 5 is the beauty, harmony, rest, and satisfaction after the storm. Act 4 is the storm. The Christian group is threatened by one who is alien to its principles. No one can deny the theatrical effectiveness of Act 4, the climax of the play, its exciting melodrama. But it *is* a parable, and its characters *are* symbolic. Portia is not merely Bassanio's clever young wife in disguise. She is allegory, the voice of God, the epitome of the New Law. Shylock too is symbol. He, new-destructive, is really a harking back to the old and pre-Christ. Shylock is the Old Law. He is the letter rather than the spirit. He is legalized injustice. He is hatred and inhumanity. He is the nihilism of selfish economic aggrandizement unmasked—as criminally destructive as murder. He is most frightening because he has law on his side. (In 1571, usury of not more than 10 percent became legal in England.) The community, it seems, must not only tolerate the enemy of good society these

26

days, but, as it were, aid him to achieve his ends. Usury is legal, and Shylock's bond is legal—but they are not *moral*. The difference between the Tudor period and the later seventeenth century is that economic vice, legalized or not, had not yet been sanctified into social virtue.

The Duke calls Shylock, who has not yet come on, an "inhuman wretch" because he is void of "pity" and "mercy." Shylock enters. The Duke emphasizes the Jew's "strange" cruelty. He hopes that Shylock "touch'd with humane gentleness and love" will forgive Antonio not only his life but repayment of the money. The Duke expects a "gentle answer." But Shylock, emphasizing the legality of his position, refuses to give a *rational* answer as to why he wants Antonio's "carrion flesh." It is his "humour," his "affection"; it is a "certain loathing," and he refuses double payment of the loan.

*Duke:* How shalt thou hope for mercy, rend'ring none?
*Shylock:* What judgment shall I dread, doing no wrong?

Thus, the Duke, *before* Portia, invokes "measure for measure." But the law-protected Shylock foresees no punishment either on earth or in after-life. He has no sense of sin or shame for what he is doing.

While the Duke converses apart with Nerissa dressed as a lawyer's clerk, Shylock takes out his knife and whets it on the sole of his shoe. Gratiano's outbreak at this spectacle stresses the non-humanity of the Jew. Shylock scoffs, "I stand here for law." Then Portia enters as a Doctor of Laws. She tells Shylock that his suit is of "a strange nature," yet Venetian law "Cannot impugn you as you do proceed." Hence, she declares, "must the Jew be merciful." "On what compulsion must I?" asks Shylock. It is not law but humanity that must rule you, replies Portia. Mercy is above justice. But Shylock is obdurate.

27

He again invokes "measure for measure" treatment: "My deeds upon my head! I crave the law. . . ." He hypocritically refuses repayment: "An oath, an oath, I have an oath in heaven!" Again Portia appeals to him: "Be merciful./Take thrice thy money; bid me tear the bond." Again Shylock invokes the law:

> I charge you by the law,
> Whereof you are a well-deserving pillar,
> Proceed to judgment.

And yet once more Shylock refuses "charity" and reads the law narrowly and inhumanly:

*Portia:* Have by some surgeon, Shylock, on your charge,
  To stop his wounds, lest he do bleed to death.
*Shylock:* Is it so nominated in the bond?
*Portia:* It is not so express'd; but what of that?
  'Twere good you do so much for charity.
*Shylock:* I cannot find it; 'tis not in the bond.

Antonio is spiritually ready: "I am arm'd and well prepar'd." Bassanio and Gratiano say that they would sacrifice their wives to save Antonio. In an aside, Shylock sneers at these "Christian husbands."

Note that Shylock has been given opportunity again and again to be merciful—and to be well paid in the bargain, too. But he has refused to forego cannibalism. He has constantly appealed to the law. So, when the law turns on him, he is the logical recipient of the eye-for-an-eye code. If he takes one drop of Antonio's blood, Portia declares, his lands and goods are "by the laws of Venice confiscate." Suddenly, the Jew (despite his oath!) is willing to take thrice repayment and forget the bond. No, says Portia, let the inhuman interpreter of the letter of the law proceed now according to the letter—but if he take more than a fraction of a fraction of a pound, he him-

28

self must die and his estate will be seized. *Now* Shylock will be satisfied with his principal. No, says Portia, follow the law and take your forfeiture of the flesh. Shylock, caught, gives up the bond snarlingly and prepares to leave. But the law which he has invoked so often has a terrible claim on him. If an "alien" has attempted the life of a "citizen," he loses all his goods (one-half to the would-be victim, one-half to the state), and his life is at the mercy of the state.

This is the ethical crux of the play. How vicious throughout *The Merchant of Venice* the Christians are to the Jew, say most of the critics. Well, here is the test. The Jew was merciless to the Christians. How will the Christians act now that they have Shylock on the hip? Portia advises him, "Down, therefore, and beg mercy of the Duke." But the Duke forestalls him: "That thou shalt see the difference of our spirit,/I pardon thee thy life before thou ask it." But half of his wealth is to go to Antonio, "The other half comes to the general state,/Which humbleness may drive unto a fine." Observe that the state is not at all anxious to take its legal half. But what about the other half? Legally, it belongs to Antonio. Portia turns to him, "What mercy can you render him, Antonio?" She is putting Antonio's Christianity to the severest proof. Remember that he is in judgment on one who a moment before was ready to literally cut his heart out. This is Antonio's answer:

> So please my lord the Duke and all the court
> To quit the fine for one half of his goods,
> I am content; so he will let me have
> The other half in use, to render it
> Upon his death unto the gentleman
> That lately stole his daughter—
> Two things provided more: that, for this favour,
> He presently become a Christian;

> The other, that he do record a gift
> Here in the court of all he dies possess'd
> Unto his son Lorenzo and his daughter.

The legal phrase *in use* means that Antonio will manage one-half of Shylock's property until the latter's death. The inference is that he will turn over the profits to the final possessors, Jessica and Lorenzo. (At the end of the play, after Portia gives Antonio the letter announcing the safe arrival of certain of his supposedly lost ships, he cries, "Sweet lady, you have given me life and living.") Thus Antonio takes nothing for himself. And Shylock actually loses nothing. He retains his life. And he retains all his property in that it will go to those who under any circumstances have the legal and ethical right to inherit. And Shylock has the completely free use of one-half of his apparently ample wealth. Certainly this is mercy, not cold justice!

But what about Shylock's becoming a Christian? It is hard for moderns to see that this request is also part of the Christian mercy. Only if the Jew is baptized can he escape the eternal pains of hell. As the Jew wished to kill the goodness which is Antonio, so Antonio wishes to kill the Old Adam which is in Shylock.

Times have changed. One has to adopt an historical perspective for *The Merchant of Venice* in order not to be shocked by what today seems sentimentally chauvinistic Christianity and nasty obdurate anti-Semitism. Shakespeare wrote a meaningful fantasy about a bad ogre who tried to hurt some good people in the City of God, but Jews today are so real that they can be seized and burnt in Nazi crematoria. But what Shakespeare's Jew and Shakespeare's Antonio ethically stand for is, perhaps, also real today. And some may say that this is a conflict which must go on until the last man is exterminated by the hydrogen bomb. The tendency of the modern psyche to exculpate Shylock because he is forced by society to be what he is is to misunderstand the tenor of the whole play. To Shakespeare and his audience sociological determinism was never a valid cause. It was always a villain's excuse.

# 2

## Albany

*M*any regard themselves, and want us to regard them, as professional on the subject of that species of drama conveniently covered by the term *tragedy*. Listen, they say, and we shall tell you what *Agamemnon* or *Othello* is about. But it is my view that the actual spiritual economics of a particular tragedy is not easy to apprehend or to grasp. Is there gain or loss in *Macbeth*? Gain in what, loss in what? Because we are what we are, pain and death are focal, and we cannot help recalling *King Lear* as the blinding of Gloucester and the death of Cordelia, as though these had constituted the totality of our reactions to the play. But we also sometimes remember that always at the end of every Shakespeare tragedy there is a kind of recovery. The least emotional reaction we have had, then, *at that moment,* is that the preceding events *were* terrible but they are *now* over. However, I have always felt that this is too simple, not completely true to our experience of the tragedy. Our final ease in the theatre or in the armchair,

I think we all have it to a greater or lesser degree, is due to some realization, conscious in a greater or lesser degree, that *all* that has happened in the drama we have just witnessed or read was not depressing. Sometimes it is the spiritual growth of the protagonist or an enemy—Macbeth or Macduff—that we sense or acknowledge. Sometimes it is the ineluctable surprise that evil seems productive of good, that the worse the degradation of humanity on the stage, the greater the consequent exaltation. Shockingly, blood and pain and death and betrayal appear to be the dung that makes the flower grow. How great Emilia is in the last act of *Othello*. But she would have remained a menial, the play seems to say, had no destruction occurred. Watch her as she develops stature, depth, complexity, courage: she becomes more real, more fine, as the scenes break and darken around her. Therefore I ask: Does anyone dare to say that Emilia's final apotheosis is not worth Desdemona's death?—Or that Albany's growth from nonentity to greatness in *King Lear* is not worth Gloucester's eyes? I hope I am not so stupid as to give an answer to these impossible questions. I am merely demanding that before one comes to absolute convictions about Shakespeare's tragic macrocosm he stare sufficiently long at the coarse fingers and the coarse balances he is employing.

I think the lack of comment on Albany in discussions of *King Lear* is probably due to the complexity of the play. Yet he bulks so large finally in the plot that what he is and what he signifies cannot safely be disregarded. But Shakespeare has deliberately made our progressive knowledge of him difficult. As with Emilia, we do not at first know with Albany whether we are witnessing a weak character or a lightly sketched characterization, which the dramatist will not deepen till it suits his purpose. That is, because he appears for so

long to possess no color at all, we do not definitely know till
the fourth act where to put Goneril's husband—whether with
the black characters (Goneril, Regan, Cornwall, etc.) or with
the white or relatively white (Kent, Lear, Gloucester, etc.).
But if in order to see the operation of the whole drama better,
we temporarily disengage a part of the design to study it more
closely, we shall see that Albany was meant by Shakespeare
to be observed carefully. Such observation may be both simple
and not simple. We can be satisfied merely with observing him
when he appears. Or we can never for a moment forget that
he is Cornwall's counterpart. (The grouping and the splitting
of groups are important devices in the dramatic technique of
*King Lear*.) We start with two bad daughters, Goneril and
Regan. We start, in the first scene, with their two wholly un-
portrayed husbands. Relatively soon, in 2.1, we discover what
Cornwall is. Concerning him and Regan we feel as we feel
concerning him and Edmund, that evil innately chooses evil,
that it likes it and prefers it. But what about his counterpart,
Albany? Is he choosing Goneril's viciousness? being de-
molished by it? or sitting on a fence while the new scythe
sweeps its way? Because he is a prominent but not immediately
perceivable part of the play's architecture, because Shakespeare
at first purposefully makes him two-dimensional (if "one-
dimensional" would not be a better word for his weak impression), because at times the play appears to utilize him (that is,
he does apparently what the play requires, not what he as a
character might choose), Albany is by no means the easiest
to write about of the imitations of human beings in *King Lear*.

Albany is mentioned in the first line of the play, which
actually poses the problem of his qualities versus Cornwall's.
Gloucester tells Kent that Lear seems to be still pondering
which of the two dukes is preferable. But although the play

begins with this question, although the first scene defines the daughters, defines the king, defines Kent, France, and Burgundy, it does not tell us anything conclusive about the two dukes. The scene does suggest that Albany and Cornwall must have or should have moral and psychological problems arising from the nature of the strong, forceful, bad woman to whom each is married. Is the moral grouping to be Goneril-Regan? Or Goneril-Albany plus Regan-Cornwall? Or what? It is dramatically significant that the dukes share one line, "Dear Sir forbear," when Lear seems about to strike Kent with his sword. It is also significant that the king treats them as one:

> Our son of Cornwall,
> And you our no less loving son of Albany,
> We have this hour a constant will to publish
> Our daughters' several dowers, that future strife
> May be prevented now.

and

> Cornwall and Albany,
> With my two daughters' dowers, digest the third.

Gloucester's remark on his entrance in 1.2 that "France in choler parted" is not unconnected with our memory of the first scene, that the King of France stood up against destructive egocentric power, whereas the Dukes of Cornwall and Albany remained uncommitted, or, rather, willy-nilly because of Lear's largess appeared committed—and to the viewpoint of their wives as well. But sufficient particularities for any decision concerning either duke have not as yet been given.

We first are able to measure Albany's stature in 1.3. He is not prepossessing. Goneril has been treating Lear like a bad child, has lied insufferably about the manners of his retinue, has threatened to reduce his train—and the king is wild with

36

anger. Albany enters. Lear immediately asks, "Is it your will, speak sir?" but not waiting for a reply, turns to one of his knights and orders horses to be saddled. Albany does not know at all what has just been occurring. (Why not? We have heard earlier in the scene from one of Lear's retainers that "there's a great abatement of kindness" not only in Goneril and the dependants but "in the Duke himself also.") He begs Lear to "be patient." The king does not even listen deeply to him but begins to curse Goneril, "Detested kite," etc. Albany at this outbreak seems truly perturbed but also woefully un-dominant:

*Albany:* My Lord, I am guiltless, as I am ignorant
  Of what has moved you.
*Lear:* It may be so, my Lord.

And Lear continues to curse his daughter. After his exit,

*Albany:* Now Gods that we adore, whereof comes this?
*Goneril:* Never afflict yourself to know more of it:
  But let his disposition have that scope
  As dotage gives it.

Note that neither the king nor his daughter grant Albany the character status which each acknowledges, however malevo-lently, in the other. We get the same pattern again when Lear re-enters.

*Lear:* What fifty of my followers at a clap?
  Within a fortnight?
*Albany:* What's the matter, sir?
*Lear:* I'll tell thee: life and death, I am asham'd
  That thou [Goneril] hast power to shake my manhood
    thus. . . .

The negative, uninformed, inconsiderable husband, whom the situation portrays as powerless, is brushed aside here by con-fronting father and daughter. After Lear's departure,

37

*Albany:* I cannot be so partial Goneril
  To the great love I bear you.
*Goneril:* Pray you content. What, Oswald, hoa!

As Goneril speaks bitterly about the danger of Lear's hundred knights and calls for her steward again, Shakespeare underscores her husband's non-intervention:

*Albany:* Well, you may fear too far.
*Goneril:* Safer than trust too far;
  Let me still take away the harms I fear. . . .

Note the "me" in the last line above, while remembering that the man before you is the presumptive ruler of half of England! After giving orders to Oswald, Goneril turns to her mate:

                        No, no, my Lord,
    This milky gentleness, and course of yours
    Though I condemn not, yet under pardon
    You are much more at task for want of wisdom,
    Than prais'd for harmful mildness.
*Albany:* How far your eyes may pierce, I cannot tell;
  Striving to better, oft we mar what's well.
*Goneril:* Nay then—
*Albany:* Well, well, th'event.

This man, we are ready to affirm, may be good, but he appears a weakling; there is no strength in him, no impulse to lead or control. He is dominated by his wife.

We do not see him again until 4.2, when most of the evil in the play has been accomplished. And therein lies the reason for his non-appearance. For when we are allowed to observe him once more, he will be very different. He will be shown as one whom the fact of evil is changing from a negative personality into a positive one, who is now the psychological and moral equal of his wife. But though he is not on the stage in

38

the interim, his now revealed terrible counterpart, Cornwall, is, but not allowing *his* terrible mate, Regan, to dominate; and Albany's terrible mate, Goneril, is, too, doing whatever her fiend-like nature wishes—and some query in us, some place, must be wondering where Albany is; what he would say and do *now,* facing the evil wrought by the above three and Edmund; whether and when he will return and with what characteristics. That he has not accompanied Goneril to Gloucester's castle accentuates his nonentity. But as often with Shakespeare, artifice accompanies the art. Both negatively and positively there are reasons why Albany cannot appear in the events in Gloucester's home. *Negatively:* To have Albany there would mean that he would, one way or another, have to declare himself morally; he could not evade decision before the treatment of Lear and Gloucester. For him to acquiesce in any way would make the dramatist's later particular use of him impossible; he could never be transmuted into decency. For him to object in any way would impede the mode of the play; evil is not to have a single let in *King Lear* until Gloucester's eyes are ejected—when the servant gives Cornwall a death wound. *Positively:* Shakespeare utilizes the fact of Albany, but not his character, to illustrate the consequences of Lear's fatuousness in dividing the kingdom "that future strife/May be prevented now." Albany's reported disagreement with Cornwall does nothing, I believe, to establish the former's moral superiority. For one thing, most of what we hear about it in 2.1 occurs *before* we discover what Cornwall really is. No, it is there for the play's pattern, not for characterization. In the above scene, Curan tells Edmund of "ear-kissing" rumors of "likely wars toward 'twixt the Dukes." Edmund utilizes this information in getting Edgar to flee. And Cornwall seems to be referring to future strife when he seizes upon

39

Edmund because "Natures of such deep trust, we shall much need." The next reference to the dukes' quarrels, in the first of the storm scenes, 3.1, does come perilously near to placing a cooperative Albany in the category of the greatly evil. Kent is speaking to the Gentleman, whom he is sending to Dover:

> There is division
> (Although as yet the face of it is cover'd
> With mutual cunning) 'twixt Albany, and Cornwall:
> Who have, as who have not, that their great stars
> Thron'd and set high, servants, who seem no less,
> Which are to France the spies and speculations,
> Intelligent of our state. What hath been seen,
> Either in snuffs, and packings of the Dukes,
> Or the hard rein which both of them have borne
> Against the old kind King; or something deeper,
> Whereof (perchance) these are but furnishings;
> But true it is, from France there comes a power. . . .

"Both of them!" Is Shakespeare implying that in the circumstances Albany's non-assertiveness is as criminal as Cornwall's action? I don't pretend to clarity on the problem, though I am inclined to think that Albany's character is still not involved, that artifice is employing his name and position for plot purposes. (However, when we approach the end of the play and find Albany on the side against Lear and Cordelia, a position that *perhaps* raises important moral issues, we *may* remember the above puzzling lines.) The last reference to the dukes' quarrel is in 3.3, in Gloucester's revelation to Edmund:

> Go to; say you nothing. There is division betwixt the Dukes, and a worse matter than that: I have received a letter this night, 'tis dangerous to be spoken, I have lock'd the letter in my closet, these injuries the King now bears, will be revenged home; there is part of a power already footed, we must incline to the King.

40

Coming as it does immediately after Gloucester's account of Regan and Cornwall's "unnatural dealing," this glance at the dukes' opposition might be taken as implying, once more, Albany's superiority, but I don't think this would be justified. It is again the ironic motif of internal conflict, which, as in Kent's speech, is now supplying a cause for France's invasion.

In 3.7 when Cornwall tells Edmund to travel back with Goneril, he seems to take Albany for granted concerning France's army: "Advise the Duke where you are going to a most festinate preparation."

In 4.2, after a length of time, after we have supped full of terror, pain, and pity, we meet Goneril's husband once more. And, as sometimes happens in Shakespeare, he possesses full emotional knowledge, if not the factual knowledge, of the terrible scenes which we, the spectators, have witnessed but which he has not. It is these preceding scenes that, finally, have been decisive in Albany's moral constitution. Within the *King Lear* tragic world there has occurred a melioristic phenomenon of the utmost spiritual importance. That which was weak and ineffective has been changed through the very fact of evil itself into something ethically aware and strong—but not quite yet in active leadership. Albany's transformation is recorded at the very beginning of the scene. In the presence of Edmund, Goneril asks Oswald where her "mild husband" is.

*Steward:* Madam within, but never man so chang'd:
   I told him of the army that was landed:
   He smil'd at it. I told him you were coming,
   His answer was, the worse. Of Gloucester's treachery,
   And of the loyal service of his son
   When I inform'd him, then he call'd me sot,
   And told me I had turn'd the wrong side out:
   What most he should dislike, seems pleasant to him;
   What like, offensive.

41

Goneril, now totally attracted to her husband's opposite, Edmund, reacts with lines that come uncomfortably close to the Albany whom we have hitherto observed:

> It is the cowish terror of his spirit
> That dares not undertake: he'll not feel wrongs
> Which tie him to an answer.

How sardonic is her irony concerning him when she says farewell to her lover: "I must change names at home, and give the distaff/Into my husband's hands." For to such as Goneril, Oswald's account of Albany but denotes the latter's usual weakness. We see presently how wrong she is. The steward's words, "Madam, here comes my Lord," are prescient. His first words destroy Goneril's domination forever. She is "not worth the dust which the rude wind/Blows in [her] face." One who has rejected her parent as she has "must wither,/And come to deadly use." These words are packed. Goneril is not to be trusted in any human relationship—toward husband, toward sister, toward herself. Of course she is incapable of understanding the "wisdom and goodness" which are directing his present speech. She and Regan are "vile," "filths," "tigers," "most barbarous, most degenerate." Their father is a "gracious aged man," to be treated with "reverence." Albany is certainly feeling the wrongs which have tied him to an answer! And in the clearest manner now he makes the moral distinction between himself and Cornwall:

> Could my good brother suffer you to do it?
> A man, a Prince, by him so benefited. . . .

By appealing to the "heavens . . . to tame this vile offence," Albany for the first time, but not the last, shows his great piety. Goneril sneers at him as "milk-liver'd," "a moral fool," but he refuses to consider, at this moment, her emphasis on

France's threat. He will not stop speaking of her fiendish behavior toward her father. She laughs at his "manhood—mew!" To her he is still a weakling. When the messenger tells Albany that Cornwall has been slain while putting out Gloucester's eyes, he has not a word of pity for Cornwall, only for his victim. And he prayerfully recognizes the heavenly justice in this quick striking down. The messenger's information concerning Edmund's role in this "wickedness" to his father prompts him to exclaim:

Gloucester, I live
To thank thee for the love thou show'dst the King,
And to revenge thine eyes.

So ends this significant scene.

Now how much the play requires us to pay attention to Albany's queer moral dilemma—loving Lear but yet fighting Cordelia and her army who are there for Lear's rescue—I do not know. There is some stress on this, but not enough to make it a certain central issue. Perhaps, Shakespeare's shortness with the problem is evidence that the exigencies of plot are paramount. Albany's reluctance is mentioned at the beginning of 4.5:

*Regan:* But are my brother's powers set forth?
*Steward:* Ay Madam.
*Regan:* Himself in person there?
*Steward:* Madam with much ado:
    Your sister is the better soldier.

This is the scene that announces the splitting of the sisters' attachment: they are now rivals for Edmund, but Regan does not seem to trust Albany as an efficacious stay to Goneril's wishes. And we are strongly reminded of Albany's negative culpability by Lear's words in his great mad scene, 4.6:

43

> It were a delicate stratagem to shoe
> A troop of horse with felt: I'll put't in proof,
> And when I have stol'n upon these son-in-laws,
> Then, kill, kill, kill, kill, kill, kill.

Contrariwise, we are reminded of Albany's goodness by Edgar, after he has read Goneril's murder letter to Edmund:

> O undistinguish'd space of woman's will,
> A plot upon her virtuous husband's life. . . .

Just before we see Albany again in 5.1, his irresolution in the present war situation is once more noted:

> *Bastard:* Know of the Duke if his last purpose hold,
> Or whether since he is advis'd by aught
> To change the course; he's full of alteration,
> And self-reproving; bring his constant pleasure.

Albany's solution is given to the sisters and Edmund in his first speech:

> Our very loving sister, well be-met:
> Sir, this I heard, the King is come to his daughter
> With others, whom the rigour of our state
> Forc'd to cry out: Where I could not be honest
> I never yet was valiant, for this business
> It touches us, as France invades our land.
> Not bolds the King, with others whom I fear,
> Most just and heavy causes make oppose.

I have never found this a wholly satisfactory explanation, and I can only repeat my point, that the plot needs Albany on a side to which morally, being what he is now, he simply cannot belong. It may be too, though I am reluctant to suggest this, that the theme of the invasion of England was so offensive to an English audience of Shakespeare's time, the dramatist could rely on the spectators' not questioning Albany's position. Edgar, too, seems involved in a similar necessity of plot. We

44

hear him in 5.1, after giving Goneril's epistle to her husband, speaking to Albany as though the victory of the anti-Cordelia army, i.e., Albany's, was necessary for his own settling of accounts with Edmund (as the unknown "champion"). (Is it that the destruction of the Goneril-Edmund-Regan trio has to come from *within* the group, to emanate from the leadership of Albany, who will call on Edgar?) However, when just before the battle, 5.2, Edgar tells his father, "Pray that the right may thrive," I confess I do not know to which army he is referring. And when, soon after, he announces "King Lear hath lost," it sounds as though he is speaking of his own side! But 5.3, one of the greatest suspense scences in drama, fully, I assert, justifies whatever machination Shakespeare has been employing. In this scene, the necessity of an Albany who is militarily on one side, morally on the other, is more than fully excusable. The same can be said of Edgar.

We had wondered in 5.1, before the battle, about the conjunction of Albany and Edmund as leaders of the British. We had not forgotten the former's promise to revenge Gloucester. What would be the final outcome of the relationship between the two? Edmund had tended to dismiss the other as any real difficulty:

> Now then, we'll use
> His countenance for the battle, which being done,
> Let her who would be rid of him, devise
> His speedy taking off. As for the mercy
> Which he intends to Lear and to Cordelia,
> The battle done, and they within our power,
> Shall never see his pardon: for my state
> Stands on me to defend, not to debate.

But the Albany who enters in 5.3 has a markedly increased spiritual stature. He is now, and feels he is, the one dominant

45

figure on the stage—and convinces us immediately, too. I find my own reaction to Albany's intense irony to Goneril in this scene quite meaningful. It is not until Albany is able himself to speak scornfully to this woman, who has spoken so scornfully of and to him, that I acknowledge myself wholly satisfied with his conduct. It is as though he were taking over a power which the evil group have hitherto arrogated to themselves. Albany's first words to Edmund are semi-satirical:

> Sir, you have show'd to-day your valiant strain
> And Fortune led you well.

He demands of Edmund this day's captives, Lear and Cordelia, concerning whose fate we are much on edge after the Bastard's murderous instructions to the Captain. "I do require them of you," says Albany. This man is not to be trifled with. Edmund makes an excuse,

> The question of Cordelia and her father
> Requires a fitter place.

But Albany at last and for all time puts the conscienceless fortune-seeker in his proper niche:

> Sir, by your patience,
> I hold you but a subject of this war,
> Not as a brother.

As, then, Regan and Goneril quarrel, with obvious jealousy, concerning Edmund's status, Albany watches, perhaps ironically smiling at his wife's effrontery. Finally, she cannot contain herself:

*Goneril:* Mean you to enjoy him?
*Albany:* The let-alone lies not in your good will.
*Bastard:* Nor in thine, Lord.
*Albany:* Half-blooded fellow, yes.

46

No more are words or acts to deter this strong leader, who is gladdening our hearts. He immediately arrests Edmund for treason—and scornfully reveals that he is aware of Goneril's adulterous love. She tries to speak scorn herself: "An interlude," but Albany *this time* turns his back on her and orders Edmund to defend himself in trial by combat; if a champion does not appear, Albany himself will fight him. And by "many treasons," Albany must mean not merely what Edmund intended to Albany but also what he did to Gloucester and was accessory in doing to Lear. Albany, now acting the sole authority, tells Edmund,

> Trust to thy single virtue, for thy soldiers
> All levied in my name, have in my name
> Took their discharge.

When Edmund falls to Edgar's sword, Albany exclaims, "Save him, save him." This is not pity. Albany wants Edmund to live long enough to confess. And he shows the incriminating letter to both the dying man and Goneril. She, this is most effective on Shakespeare's part, underlines the tremendous transformation that has occurred in Albany by asserting *now* that she can destroy the letter if she wishes, *now* when her husband has wholly taken over the power she once possessed:

> Say if I do, the Laws are mine not thine,
> Who can arraign me for't?

Albany, knowing how "desperate" she is, sends someone to "govern her" after her exit. The word *govern!* He embraces the revealed Edgar: "Let sorrow split my heart if ever I/Did hate thee, or thy father." And Edgar replies, "Worthy Prince, I know't." At Edgar's account of himself and Gloucester, Albany evinces deep and tender sensitivity:

47

> If there be more, more woeful, hold it in,
> For I am almost ready to dissolve,
> Hearing of this.

But the fineness of his ethos is, perhaps, best displayed by his speech after the Gentleman rushes in and tells of the sister's deaths:

> Produce the bodies, be they alive or dead;
> This judgement of the Heavens that makes us tremble,
> Touches us not with pity.

Aristotle himself could not have been more discriminating in moral reactions.

It is at this moment that the leadership of Albany in this scene is peculiarly emphasized. It was upon him that the saving of Lear and Cordelia depended, but his initial concern was put in abeyance by the necessity of dealing with the evil trio—and so our almost unbearable apprehension for the king and his daughter had likewise temporarily to be suppressed; but our concern, I believe, is never wholly out of attention. In fact, I believe, it builds up. Now, at Kent's question on the whereabouts of Lear, Albany exclaims, "Great thing of us forgot!" But even now there is interruption as the dead daughters' bodies are brought in. After Edmund at last reveals his death plan for Lear and Cordelia, Albany cries, "Run, run, O run. . . . Haste thee for thy life." He prays for Cordelia, "The Gods defend her." His piety in this scene is noteworthy.

They are too late. At the sight of Lear with the dead Cordelia in his arms, Albany's emotions are almost beyond endurance: "Fall and cease." But his pervasive control of the scene once more asserts itself:

*Messenger:* Edmund is dead my Lord.
*Albany:* That's but a trifle here:

ALBANY

> You Lords and noble friends, know our intent,
> What comfort to this great decay may come,
> Shall be appli'd. For us we will resign,
> During the life of this old Majesty
> To him our absolute power, you to your rights,
> With boot, and such addition as your honours
> Have more than merited. All friends shall taste
> The wages of their virtue, and all foes
> The cup of their deservings.

Strength, charity, justice, lack of sentimentality are all illustrated here. And after Lear's death we see that along with Albany's moral greatness goes a corresponding humility. To Kent and Edgar he says,

> Our present business
> Is general woe; friends of my soul, you twain,
> Rule in this Realm, and the gor'd state sustain.

And this great man, great in psychological strength, great in physical power, great in speech, great in piety and morality, was the nonentity with whom the play began! And *King Lear* is often described as totally dark!

# 3

## Banquo and Edgar: Character or Function?

It is no longer the fashion for criticism to regard a Shakespeare play as a kind of *D.N.B.* volume of life portraits. We now recognize that he wrote poetic drama and that such drama is necessarily governed by pattern or design. Character, event, language, theme and image are now seen as parts of a complex architecture. Moreover, we are beginning to recognize that such poetic design enforces a non-naturalistic mode, the recognition of which must ultimately affect our view of character and characterization. It is significant, for example, that J. I. M. Stewart, while maintaining the criterion of ultimate psychological truth for Shakespeare, does not do so by postulating a realistic stage—quite the contrary. Again, W. B. C. Watkins points out that a Shakespeare character can at one moment be realistic and at another symbolic. And F. P. Wilson writes, "In *Macbeth* many characters are brought in with no attempt to make them individual: the sergeant, the messenger, the doctor, the waiting-woman, the murderers, the Old Man, and we may add Ross, Angus and Lennox. The core of the play's experience is expressed through Macbeth, and these characters are without personality as much as characters in a morality play. They act as chorus to the 'swelling act of the imperial theme!' " (*Elizabethan and Jacobean*, 1945, p. 122.) But neither *chorus* nor *symbol* is a completely satisfactory term. The first tends to disallow both those touches of individualism in which the lavish Shakespeare excels and also any involvement of the character in the action; the second implies *unity* of significance and hence cannot cover a character who possesses little realistic unity and yet has a multiplicity of *ideational* purposes. I prefer the term *function*, loose as it is. It allows the critic the necessary breadth when dealing with the characterization in a Shakespeare play.

## I

If we consider Banquo as a dramatic function rather than as a character in the usual sense, we shall be able to avoid Bradley's erroneous and confusing misreading of him as another whom the witches' influence finally debases (*Shakespearean Tragedy*, 1937 ed., pp. 379 ff). Bradley, with his customary approach, tended to consider Banquo as a whole man, a psychologically valid being; he did not see that the playwright has so depicted the character that he will always be a dramaturgic foil to Macbeth.

As Banquo and Macbeth meet the witches in 1.3, Banquo notes that Macbeth "start[s]" and "seem[s] to fear" the witches' prophecies, that he "seems rapt withal"; but by his bold words to them, Banquo indicates that *he* has a free soul, "who neither beg nor fear/Your favors nor your hate." Again,

52

when Ross calls Macbeth Thane of Cawdor, it is Banquo who
once and for all clearly indicates to the audience the true nature
of the witches: "What, can the devil speak true?" Although
Banquo suspects nothing of Macbeth's intentions, he does
know the nature of man and of Satan:

> And oftentimes to win us to our harm,
> The instruments of darkness tell us truths,
> Win us with honest trifles, to betray's
> In deepest consequence.

Hence, he already knows what Macbeth does not learn completely until the very end: he has immediately recognized the
witches as cunning emissaries of the enemy of mankind. And
it is significant that Macbeth immediately wants to win
Banquo to his side: "let us speak/Our free hearts each to
other." *Free* means *open* as well as *innocent*. Banquo replies, "Very gladly." The ease of the answer indicates once
more a truly free heart. So, already, Shakespeare's pattern is
emerging; Macbeth, tempted by evil, feels a strong desire to
negate the difference which Banquo stands for.

In 1.5, Lady Macbeth prays (I mean this word literally) the
"murth'ring ministers" to unsex her. Begging the devil to
deprive her of the ordinary human qualities of pity and remorse, she requests the "dunnest smoke of hell" in which to
commit the crime. It is meaningfully to Banquo in 1.6 that
Shakespeare gives the lines describing Inverness castle in semi-
religious terms—"temple-haunting martlet," "heaven's breath,"
"pendent bed and procreant cradle." We are meant to feel
deeply here the contrast between Banquo's vision and the
devil-haunted castle of actuality. The next scene, 1.7, shows
us a Macbeth who almost seems to have felt the implications
of those words of Banquo:

> [Duncan's] virtues
> Will plead like angels, trumpet-tongu'd, against
> The deep damnation of his taking off;
> And pity, like a naked new-born babe,
> Striding the blast, or heaven's cherubin, hors'd
> Upon the sightless couriers of the air,
> Shall blow the horrid deed in every eye,
> That tears shall drown the wind.

But his devil-possessed lady wins him over. And note how tightly Shakespeare has woven his pattern of contrasts: In 1.5 Lady Macbeth prayed to Satan to turn her "milk" into "gall." In 1.6 Banquo referred to the evidence of a godly home, the "procreant cradle." In 1.7 Macbeth speaks of "pity, like a naked new-born babe." Later in 1.7 Lady Macbeth says that she could snatch the smiling babe from her breast and dash its brains out!

At the beginning of Act 2, just before the entrance of Macbeth, who will leave the stage to murder Duncan, Shakespeare once more presents Banquo. In his customary manner, Banquo is aware of the supernatural powers above and below. It is a dark night: "There's husbandry in heaven;/Their candles are all out." ("Stars, hide your fires!" "Nor heaven peep through the blanket of the dark." Apparently, the demonic prayers of Macbeth and his lady have been answered.) But though the night is indeed dark, Banquo's words have, beyond his awareness, a prophetic undertone: if *husbandry* means thrift, it also means wise management. Hence, through Banquo, obliquely, the irresistible justice and omniscience of heaven is being urged. Banquo continues to Fleance, "A heavy summons lies like lead upon me,/And yet I would not sleep." The first line might suggest that the dark powers are working upon him to get him out of the way of the criminals; at any rate, his soul apprehends evil. So, being the kind of man he is, he prays to

54

the instruments of light to fight against the instruments of darkness:

> Merciful powers,
> Restrain in me the cursed thoughts that nature
> Gives way to in repose.

To Bradley, "the poison [of the witches] has begun to work," but that is not at all the purport of these lines; they are there for comparison. Everyman is constantly being tempted by evil: during waking hours, he is free to expel it from his mind; but while he and his will are asleep, the demons can invade his dreams. (Macbeth a few lines later puts the matter clearly: "wicked dreams abuse/The curtain'd sleep.") Therefore, Banquo prays for grace, for holy power outside himself to repel the demons. In contrast Macbeth and Lady Macbeth have prayed far otherwise.

After Macbeth's entrance, Banquo declares: "I dreamt last night of the three weird sisters./To you they have showed some truth." These are the "cursed thoughts" that Banquo wishes to expunge—and it is as though Banquo, as instrument rather than as character, unwittingly, is testing Macbeth. Macbeth feels this, he wants to get Banquo on his side, he wants to talk to Banquo about the witches.

*Banquo:* At your kind'st leisure.
*Macbeth:* If you shall cleave to my consent, when 'tis,
  It shall make honor for you.
*Banquo:*                 So I lose none
  In seeking to augment it but still keep
  My bosom franchis'd and allegiance clear,
  I shall be counsel'd.

Bradley found this Banquo-Macbeth colloquy "difficult to interpret." So it is, inspected as realism; but if one regards the two speakers here not so much as people but as morality play

55

figures who have chosen different sides in the struggle between Heaven and Hell, there is little difficulty. Macbeth is the representative of the Tempter, and Banquo refuses the bait, not with polite evasiveness but with formal rejection. For there is a dichotomy both in Macbeth and in Macbeth's world as long as Banquo represents the good; from Macbeth's viewpoint, Banquo must either be absorbed or destroyed if Macbeth is to gain ease.

In 2.3, when Macduff tells Banquo that their king has been murdered, Lady Macbeth cries, "Woe, alas!/What, in our house?" Banquo's reply is a semi-rebuke that comes automatically to his lips, "Too cruel anywhere." He is not hiding anything: there is such correspondence between his mind and his mouth that his three words dismiss his hostess' apparently limited morality and express a universal reaction. But Banquo is not suspicious of any single person, yet; he does not know who or what the enemy is, yet. All he knows is that he is innocent and that a great crime has been committed:

> In the great hand of God I stand, and thence
> Against the undivulg'd pretense I fight
> Of treasonous malice.

Note how the combatants in the action have been depersonalized by Banquo's words; the war between Good and Evil is larger than people.

On Banquo's next appearance, I quote Bradley:

> When next we see him, on the last day of his life, we find that he has yielded to evil. The Witches and his own ambition have conquered him. He alone of the lords knew of the prophecies, but he has said nothing of them. He has acquiesced in Macbeth's accession, and in the official theory that Duncan's sons had suborned the chamberlains to murder him. Doubtless, un-

56

like Macduff, he was present at Scone to see the new king invested. He has, not formally but in effect, 'cloven to' Macbeth's 'consent': he is knit to him by a 'most indissoluble tie'; his advice in council has been 'most grave and prosperous'; he is to be the 'chief guest' at that night's supper. And his soliloquy tells us why:

> Thou hast it now: king, Cawdor, Glamis, all,
> As the weird women promis'd, and, I fear,
> Thou play'dst most foully for't: yet it was said
> It should not stand in thy posterity,
> But that myself should be the root and father
> Of many kings. If there come truth from them—
> As upon thee, Macbeth, their speeches shine—
> Why, by the verities on thee made good,
> May they not be my oracles as well,
> And set me up in hope? But hush! no more.

This 'hush! no more' is not the dismissal of 'cursed thoughts': it only means that he hears the trumpets announcing the entrance of the King and Queen.

His punishment comes swiftly, much more swiftly than Macbeth's, and saves him from any further fall.

Surely Bradley, writing as through Banquo were an historical figure and not part of a drama, has gone astray. Act 3 begins with Macbeth king, and Banquo suspecting he played most foully for it. It is not allowable, dramatically speaking, to conjecture anything about Banquo between his last appearance and his present appearance. Furthermore, the "indissoluble tie" is that between a king and his subject, and there is nothing evil in it. The "grave and prosperous" advice is not criminal aid to the murderer but political counsel to his sovereign. As to Banquo's character and motives in regard to the crown, all the soliloquy tells us is that he anticipates great honour as the founder of a royal line. There is not a hint that he will play "most foully" to make the prophecy come true. Primarily, the soliloquy is meant to remind the audience of what the witches told Banquo two full acts back, for that promise may be said to guide the action of the play until the blood-boltered Banquo points at the show of the eight kings—and even then Macbeth's horror at this truth motivates his slaughter of Lady Macduff. As usual Shakespeare's purpose with Banquo here is not similarity but dissimilarity. Dramaturgically, Banquo *must* be maintained as contrast.

That it is not Banquo so much as person but what he still epitomizes which prompts Macbeth to kill his one-time companion is brought out, I believe, in Macbeth's famous soliloquy:

> To be thus is nothing
> But to be safely thus. Our fears in Banquo
> Stick deep, and in his royalty of nature
> Reigns that which would be fear'd. 'Tis much he dares,
> And to that dauntless temper of his mind
> He hath a wisdom that doth guide his valor
> To act in safety. There is none but he
> Whose being I do fear, and under him
> My genius is rebuk'd, as it is said
> Mark Antony's was by Caesar. He chid the sisters
> When first they put the name of king upon me
> And bade them speak to him. Then, prophet-like,
> They hail'd him father to a line of kings.
> Upon my head they plac'd a fruitless crown
> And put a barren sceptre in my gripe,
> Thence to be wrench'd with an unlineal hand,
> No son of mine succeeding. If't be so,
> For Banquo's issue have I fil'd my mind;
> For them the gracious Duncan have I murther'd;
> Put rancors in the vessel of my peace
> Only for them, and mine eternal jewel
> Given to the common enemy of man
> To make them kings, the seed of Banquo kings!

Rather than so, come fate into the list
And champion me to th' utterance!

What is it that Macbeth fears? Is it really Banquo the man?
Or is it the latter's still unsullied qualities—his natural royalty,
his dauntless temper, his wise valour? Banquo represents what
a part of Macbeth wants and, also, what a part of Macbeth
hates. He is truly, as the witches declared, both happier and
greater than the regicide. Let us put it this way: Macbeth is
jealous of Banquo's virtues, wants them but cannot have them,
feels belittled by them, fears them, and hence must destroy
them. The killing of Banquo may be interpreted as a futile
effort on Macbeth's part to destroy his own better humanity;
it is a ghastly effort to unify Macbeth's inner and outer world,
for Banquo has a daily beauty in his life that makes Macbeth
ugly. The fear of an "unlineal hand," the belief that Banquo's
issue will immediately succeed him are rationalizations, the
false coinage of an agonized man who has sold his soul to the
devil, who has exchanged his "eternal jewel" for a poisoned,
tortured mind. It is not really Banquo the person whom Macbeth fears: it is Banquo as symbol, he who stood "in the great
hand of God." [1]

Interestingly enough, the non-Bradleyan Banquo emerges
as a more dramatically effective figure if only because he is
uncomplex, consistent, and trenchant.

## II

Critics seem somewhat at a loss when dealing with Edgar.
"Edgar is the most complex of all Shakespearean parts. No
conscious conceited actor dare attempt it" (J. Isaacs, "Shakespeare as Man of the Theatre," in *Shakespeare Criticism 1919-35*,
ed. Anne Bradby, 1941, p. 311). "And the notion of that

strange disguise [of Poor Tom] would not come, we may say, to a commonplace man. . . . 'Bear free and patient thoughts,' he tells his father, when, by his queer stratagem [in the Dover Cliff scene]—again it was not the notion of a commonplace mind—he has saved him from despair. His playing the peasant with the insufferable Oswald is, yet again, not commonplace . . ." (H. Granville-Barker, *Prefaces to Shakespeare,* 1946, I, 319-20). "There was no reason for Edgar to play the peasant, but Shakespeare's audience must have been amused and pleased to see a country fellow armed only with a cudgel, Edgar's 'ballow,' knock down and kill the overweening retainer [Oswald] of a great lord, a type heartily disliked by London citizens" (T. M. Parrott, *Shakespearean Comedy,* 1949, p. 300).

With our very strong present-day propensity towards psychological consistency in the theatre, with our tendency always to see action as the result of character, we are not properly conditioned to see both character and action as interrelated aspects of a larger poetic design. When we think of Edgar *qua* Edgar, we tend to think of the noble, tender-hearted, but just, stoical being who utters aphorisms:

> When we our betters see bearing our woes,
> We scarcely think our miseries our foes.

> The lamentable change is from the best;
> The worst returns to laughter.

> Men must endure
> Their going hence, even as their coming hither;
> Ripeness is all.

> The gods are just, and of our pleasant vices
> Make instruments to plague us.

60

Yet the Edgar who thus appears to us occupies a very small proportion of the lines, prefixed *Edgar,* in the play. How does one correlate the seasoned stoic with the Edgar whom Edmund easily dupes at the beginning of the play?

> . . . a brother noble,
> Whose nature is so far from doing harms
> That he suspects none, on whose foolish honesty
> My practices ride easy.

(The concealed image is that of an ass.) With the Edgar who is Poor Tom? With the Edgar of the Dover Cliff scene? With the dialect-speaking peasant who kills Oswald? And, possibly, there are still other Edgars who provide the ending of the play by revealing Goneril's letter to Albany and by overcoming Edmund.

To make a psychological unity of these various roles is, I think, misguided endeavour. These roles are not products of a mind that is not "commonplace." The mind that is not commonplace is Shakespeare's. Edgar is not a mimetic unity; he is a dramatic device. Each of his roles contributes not to a rich psychological unity but to Shakespeare's poetic purposes. True, Edgar has a basic plot function, that of being the dispossessed son. But his various roles do not tell us more about Edgar. They tell us more about the play in which he is a character. There is a critical touchstone concerning Edgar's functionalism: Kent in disguise is still fundamentally the same character as Kent not in disguise.

Altogether, before he exists at 2.1.32, a hunted criminal, Edgar speaks less than sixty words. Of these, less than thirty-five are his rejoinders to Edmund's questions about his relations with his father. And none of these thirty-five indicate anything more than total belief in Edmund. It takes Edmund from 1.2.144 to 1.2.169 to convince him that Gloucester is mortally angry at him and that he should hide in Edmund's quarters. After Edmund calls to him to descend at 2.1.19 and asks him whether he has taken Albany's side against Cornwall, Edgar merely makes a denial of seven words. Edmund then tells him to draw and fight—Edgar silently does what he is told to do—and then flees. Is Edgar a nincompoop? Not at all. Clearly, we are here in the presence of a theatrical convention —a character's being precipitated into action by the dramatist rather than being motivated into action by psychology. Shakespeare makes the two scenes go very fast precisely because he doesn't want us to have time to weigh probability. And he largely escapes the problem of probability by not characterizing Edgar at all. One cannot say the character is improbable; properly speaking, there is no character—there is only a puppet.

When Edgar reappears in 2.3, he has decided, in order to escape capture, to disguise himself as a mad beggar, Poor Tom. His last words in this soliloquy are pertinent: "Edgar I nothing am." But if he is not Edgar, what is he? Without pretending to be comprehensive, I suggest that the role of Poor Tom has four major functions, which are, of course, not mutually exclusive: to provide spectacle, to be a component of Lear's re-education, to enforce the religious querying running throughout the play, and to contrast with Oswald.

The title-page of the 1608 quarto singles out for advertisement only one of the subsidiary characters: "With the unfortunate life of Edgar, sonne and heire to the Earle of Gloster, and his sullen and assumed humor of Tom of Bedlam." So Tom must have caught the attention of the spectators. The text indicates his appearance: no clothing except a blanket around his middle, disordered hair, and grimed face. As he whirls through his disjointed speeches, fragments of poetry, snatches of song, we see his gestures and movements—striking at the fiend, scratching his back, wrapping his arms around himself because he is cold, hearing a voice in his belly, throwing an imaginary head. Ridiculous, grotesque and frightening, the spectacle of crazy Tom is not the least of the play's attractions.

The Lear who has such an all-compelling necessity for a hundred followers must be re-educated. Just before he goes out into the storm, the problem comes into focus. Why do you need any retinue? ask Goneril and Regan. Lear replies,

> O reason not the need! Our basest beggars     2 ems
> Are in the poorest thing superfluous;
> Allow not nature more than nature needs,
> Man's life is cheap as beast's. Thou art a lady;
> If only to go warm were gorgeous,
> Why, nature needs not what thou gorgeous wear'st,
> Which scarcely keeps thee warm. But, for true need—

Thus he breaks off without answering the great question, but his implied answer is that his true need *does* have something to do with gorgeous robes and a hundred knights. At this stage Lear is not really concerned with the basest beggars; they are only a part of his argument. It is not of their minimum needs as almost animals but of his minimum needs as a great king that he is speaking. Later, however, the storm forces him out of himself into an empathic concern for these basest beggars:

> Poor naked wretches, wheresoe'er you are,
> That bide the pelting of this pitiless storm.
> How shall your houseless heads and unfed sides,
> Your loop'd and window'd raggedness defend you
> From seasons such as these? Oh I have ta'en
> Too little care of this. Take physic pomp;
> Expose thyself to feel what wretches feel,

> That thou may'st shake the superflux to them
> And show the heavens more just.

Exposed to the savagery of the elements, Lear begins to feel a kinship with the basest beggars and a real concern for their basic needs of food, clothing and shelter. But he is still the king, and they are still poor naked wretches. They and he are separated by social status. But when Poor Tom, in his loincloth, enters, when Lear sees before him in the flesh one of the very creatures he has been postulating, Lear at last recognizes that basically he, the great king, and Poor Tom, the naked beggar, are really the same, that gorgeous robes are only sophistications which hide this inescapable truth:

> Thou wert better in a grave than to answer with thy uncovered body this extremity of the skies. Is man no more than this? Consider him well. Thou owest the worm no silk, the beast no hide, the sheep no wool, the cat no perfume. Ha, here's three on's are sophisticated! Thou are the thing itself; unaccommodated man is no more but such a poor, bare, forked animal as thou art. Off, off, you lendings! Come, unbutton here.

In attempting to strip off his clothing, Lear is attempting to assert his fundamental kinship to the bedlamite. All in all, in learning a profound lesson in the emptiness of class distinctions, in a humility that is as agonizing as it is disillusioning, Lear indeed answers the complex problem of true need. To Lear, Tom is a "noble philosopher," "learned Theban," "good Athenian" because his presence drives the king to a consideration of primacies—and Lear does not forget the lesson. Listen to him in the great mad scene of 4.6:

> When the rain came to wet me once, and the wind to make me chatter, when the thunder would not peace at my bidding, there I found 'em, there I smelt 'em out.

> Go to, they are not men o' their words; they told me
> I was everything. 'Tis a lie—I am not ague-proof.

> Thou hast seen a farmer's dog bark at a beggar?
> Ay, sir.
> And the creature run from the cur? There
> thou might'st behold the great image of authority:
> a dog's obeyed in office.

> Through tatter'd clothes great vices do appear;
> Robes and furr'd gowns hide all. Plate sin with gold,
> And the strong lance of justice hurtless breaks.
> Arm it in rags a pygmy's straw does pierce it.

So Poor Tom is an important visual correlative in Lear's reassessment of values.[2]

*King Lear* is a religious play in the sense that what happens in it drives certain of the characters—as well as the spectators, perhaps—to metaphysical probing and assertion. That it is laid in pre-Christian times need not at all mean that it is not Christian in content. But since it is a play in which religious doubts and affirmations arise within various characters who are within the flow of the action, it is better from the dramatic viewpoint that the Christian system be not authoritative and that it be one of several conflicting eschatologies. For example, Edmund says, "Thou, Nature, art my goddess." Gloucester says, "As flies to wanton boys are we to th' gods." Albany says, "This shows you are above,/You justicers, that these our nether crimes/So speedily can venge!" Edgar (as Edgar) says, "The gods are just, and of our pleasant vices/Make instruments to plague us." *King Lear* is a multiple experience out of which religion can come. It is necessary that the formal Christian viewpoint be there—but not ostensibly. Poor Tom supplies this formal viewpoint. "Pray, innocent," he exclaims, "and beware the foul fiend." That is, believe in Christ, follow

His rule, and beware the devil's temptations. The constant inference from Poor Tom's chatter is that he is damned on earth by demonic possession and persecution because of his past vicious life. He is ever-conscious of Hell. He restates the Ten Commandments. He knows the major sins by which the devil captures human souls. He knows that suicide is the unforgivable sin. He understands that pride in the carnal pleasures of the earth and the breaking of God's holy laws go before a fall. The feeling, which some people have, that *King Lear* is ultimately a Christian play, that ultimately in a profound sense it is optimistic, is not a feeling that anyone can force on anyone else. That the only formal statement of Christianity in the play is by a filthy madman is perversely arcane—and deliberately so.

There is a curious connection between Poor Tom and Oswald. I never fully realized the importance of the latter in Shakespeare's dramatic design until I saw a sensitive performance of the play. Beribboned, graceful, sophisticated and cocksure, Oswald breeds a special kind of fear in the spectator. If the faithful servitors—the Fool, Kent and Cornwall's servant —belong to the old world of faith, love, morality and decency, Oswald belongs body and soul to the new world of opportunity, selfishness, immorality and cruelty. Even more than Edmund (the complete opportunist), Oswald shows the nastiness of the new way of things. For there is a grandeur about the great evil characters: Goneril, Regan, Cornwall and Edmund; they are titanic forces as well as human characters. "The prince of darkness is a gentleman!" There is nothing small about them. Oswald, on the other hand, is petty; he is not dignified by intellect, passion, or overriding purpose; he is merely the steward who wants to make his way, who is servant to the core. Always the follower, he is always looking out for himself—a coward before the strong and a bully before the weak. His marks are compliance to the new-successful and scorn for the old-defeated. Without a background of property, breeding, or ethic, he exhibits a sordidness of choice that illustrates the disintegrating power and the absolute corruption of the Goneril-Edmund viewpoint. Representing a status in society too close to that of many in the audience, he is meant to instill in the spectator an uncomfortable disgust and terror.

Shakespeare definitely relates him to Poor Tom. "What hast thou been?" Lear asks the madman. This is the reply:

> A servingman, proud in heart and mind; that curled my hair, wore gloves in my cap; served the lust of my mistress' heart and did the act of darkness with her; swore as many oaths as I spake words, and broke them in the sweet face of heaven; one that slept in the contriving of lust, and waked to do it. Wine loved I deeply, dice dearly; and in woman outparamoured the Turk. False of heart, light of ear, bloody of hand; hog in sloth, fox in stealth, wolf in greediness, dog in madness, lion in prey. Let not the creaking of shoes nor the rustling of silks betray thy poor heart to woman. Keep thy foot out of brothels, thy hand out of plackets, thy pen from lender's books, and defy the foul fiend.

Later Poor Tom states that although now his food is rodents and his drink the scum of a standing pool; although now he is whipped, stock-punished and imprisoned, he once "Had three suits to his back, six shirts to his body, horse to ride, and weapon to wear." While leading his father, Edgar exclaims:

> Five fiends have been in Poor Tom at once: of lust, as Obidicut; Hobbididence, prince of darkness; Mahu of stealing; Modo, of murder; Flibbertigibbet, of mopping and mowing, who since possesses chambermaids and waiting women.

Let us sum up these passages. At one time Poor Tom had been a serving man, who had come up in the world from a low beginning. He tried to act like a gentleman, borrowed money, wore a sword at his side, and kept a horse. Smiling and grimacing, he acted the dandy—though he had only six shirts and the usual manservant's allowance of three suits. He put himself completely in his mistress' command. He served her lust. He swore oaths easily. He broke loyalties. He was overbearing, cowardly, and sadistic.

It is astonishing how much of this dovetails with Kent's vituperation of Oswald in 2.2:

A knave; a rascal; an eater of broken meats; a base, proud, shallow, beggarly, three-suited, hundred-pound, filthy, worsted-stocking knave; a lily-livered, action-taking, whoreson, glass-gazing, superserviceable, finical rogue; one-trunk-inheriting slave; one that would'st be a bawd in way of good service, and art nothing but the composition of a knave, beggar, coward, pander, and the son and heir of a mongrel bitch; one whom I will beat into clamorous whining, if thou deny'st the least syllable of thy addition.

That such a slave as this should wear a sword,
Who wears no honesty. Such smiling rogues as these,
Like rats, oft bite the holy cords atwain
Which are too intrinse to unloose; smooth every passion
That in the nature of their lords rebel,
Bring oil to fire, snow to the colder moods;
Renege, affirm, and turn their halcyon beaks
With every gale and vary of their masters,
Knowing naught (like dogs) but following.
A plague upon your epileptic visage!
Smile you my speeches, as I were a fool?
Goose, if I had you upon Sarum Plain,
I'ld drive ye cackling home to Camelot.

And this is how Edgar describes Oswald in 4.6:

> I know thee well. A serviceable villain,
> As duteous to the vices of thy mistress
> As badness would desire.
>
>                     the post unsanctified
> Of murtherous lechers.

(Edgar's servingman "served the lust of my mistress' heart and did the act of darkness with her." Regan intimates in 4.5 that Oswald is in the same relationship to Goneril: "I know you are of her bosom." Cf. Regan to Edmund concerning Goneril in 5.1: "I am doubtful that you have been conjunct/ and bosom'd with her.") Thus, in Shakespeare's dramatic design the courtier, Oswald, is related to the courtier-become-madman, Poor Tom. What is the point of this relationship? It is prophetic: it implies that the eternal laws still endure, that the Oswalds of this world will be destroyed. It says that Poor Tom is more sane than Oswald, that Poor Tom is more beautiful than Oswald.

In the Dover Cliff scene, Edgar is not so much Edgar as, literally, a *deus ex machina*. His rapid assumption of roles in this part of the play tends to obliterate his personal identity. When we last saw him leading his blinded father, he was a naked bedlamite. Now he is wearing a peasant costume. Gloucester notes that he is speaking "in better phrase and matter." After Gloucester jumps, Edgar asks who was with him on the "crown o' the cliff." Gloucester replies, "A poor unfortunate beggar." No, says Edgar, it was a horrible fiend, with huge eyes, many noses and twisted horns. Later Gloucester asks, "What are you?" Edgar answers:

> A most poor man, made tame to fortune's blows,
> Who, by the art of known and feeling sorrows,
> Am pregnant to good pity.

These sudden shifts force us to view Shakespeare's Edgar as a character being adapted to various dramatic purposes. What is the embracing purpose of Edgar in the Dover Cliff episode? Each of the major "good" characters in the play reacts to his evil with different capacities of endurance. Lear cries: "You heavens, give me that patience, patience I need!" But to Edgar, "Ripeness is all." Kent in the stocks says, "Nothing almost sees miracles/But misery." And Cordelia, after she and her father have been taken, declares, "For thee, oppressed king, am I cast down;/Myself could else outfrown false Fortune's frown." Violated, the once buoyant and strong Gloucester loses his capacity to go on. It is not the badness of man, merely, that has destroyed his spirit. It is his conclusion that the rulers of the universe themselves are malicious. He is still a believer; but whereas before his blinding he said, "I shall see/The winged vengeance overtake such children," after his blinding he says, "As flies to wanton boys are we to th' gods./They kill us for their sport." In a word Gloucester is possessed by "despair" (4.6.33), a paralysing disbelief in the goodness of providence. Why then should a man live? He has decided to commit suicide. This is his speech before he jumps:

> O you mighty gods!
> This world I do renounce, and, in your sights,
> Shake patiently my great affliction off.
> If I could bear it longer and not fall
> To quarrel with your great opposeless wills,
> My snuff and loathed part of nature should
> Burn itself out. If Edgar live, O bless him!

Shakespeare has caught the very essence of religious despair here: the gods can be good (let them bless Edgar), but they are implacably inimical to him, Gloucester. Only the palpable intervention of the gods, only a miracle, can restore Gloucester's faith that the gods are consistently good, that they wish him well, and that he must go on living within their mysterious plan. The miracle occurs—Gloucester is not killed by his great fall. The man beside him, who has seen the miracle, says:

> Therefore, thou happy father,
> Think that the clearest gods, who make their honours
> Of men's impossibilities, have preserved thee.

And Gloucester indicates that the miracle has taken effect,

> Henceforth I'll bear
> Affliction till it do cry out itself
> 'Enough, enough,' and die. That thing you speak of,
> I took it for a man. Often 'twould say
> 'The fiend, the fiend'—he led me to that place.

"He led me to that place." It was the power of evil that tempted him to suicide. The function of Edgar in this scene is to play a part in the spiritual rehabilitation of Gloucester: "Why I do trifle thus with his despair/Is done to cure it."

When Edgar becomes a dialect-speaking peasant who defeats the represensative of the Goneril-Edmund order, Oswald, he is playing a part within a dramatic design that began much earlier. Its recurrent motif is the problem of loyalties. Kent in opposition to his master in the first scene, the Fool who will not turn knave by running away, the Captain who obeys Edmund's command to kill Cordelia are also parts of this design. The poor, bare, forked animal runs from the dog, authority, but he can turn if the dog becomes too beastly. To be subservient to a dog is to become like a dog, like Oswald. After all, one has a loyalty to one's humanity too. And it is among the less accommodated and sophisticated that Shakespeare first shows this natural tendency operating in a way momentous for the drama. The noble and sophisticated Edmund, Regan, Goneril and Cornwall, the rulers, are inhuman. It is the sudden and unexpected appearance of basic humanity among the lowly that constitutes the turning-point in the play. Edgar has been totally dispossessed, Lear has been made a homeless madman, Gloucester is strapped in a chair, and we watch, frightened and helpless, the bloody ejection of his eye. The evil has been mighty and horrible and unstayed. It looks as though it will take over the universe.

All at once, surprisingly, out of the nameless crew of servants around Gloucester's chair, one servant disengages himself, with force prevents Cornwall from reaching Gloucester's other eye, and speaks:

> Hold you hand, my lord!
> I have serv'd you ever since I was a child;
> But better service have I never done you
> Than now to bid you hold.

The astonished Regan and Cornwall call him peasant and villain. "A peasant stand up thus?" But the servant scorns Regan, and fights Cornwall. And he dies, but not before giving Cornwall a fatal wound. Not all followers are Oswalds. This servant, with nothing to gain and everything to lose, realizes, here, that he has a deeper loyalty than that of Cornwall. It is this realization and his consequent act that represent the first defeat of evil in the play.

And Shakespeare reinforces his point. Though Cornwall orders the dead slave to be thrown on the dunghill, two other servants resolve to go against orders and aid Gloucester. They indicate that neither they nor the nature of things can tolerate the evil of Cornwall and Regan. The homely remedy! "Flax and whites of eggs." And the significant last words: "Now heaven help him!" Men are not all monsters, and there is a

72

heaven. At the moment of greatest horror, three servants teach us this.

The lesson goes on. In the next scene, a nameless Old Man helps Gloucester even though the latter warns him, "Thy conforts can do me no good at all;/Thee they may hurt." But the Old Man refuses to leave. Doing good may endanger him, but he will do it; he refuses to be inhuman. Gloucester has asked him to bring clothing for Poor Tom; the Old Man declares, "I'll bring him the best 'parel that I have,/Come on't what will." Note the faint touch of country speech. The Old Man is a peasant, "I have been your tenant, and your father's tenant,/These fourscore years." Thus, he adds a further dimension to the opposition of the lowly to the evil. He enlarges it to the opposition of the country to the court.

So the meeting of Edgar as a dialect-speaking peasant and Oswald has been poetically prepared for. Shakespeare uses Edgar here to repeat a motif significantly. Oswald sees Gloucester as a "traitor" whose death will "raise my fortunes." He pays no attention to the peasant and advances to kill the helpless old earl. But the peasant interposes. Oswald is surprised.

> Wherefore, bold peasant,
> Darest thou support a publish'd traitor. Hence,
> Lest that the infection of his fortune take
> Like hold on thee.

The new order threatens punishment to whatever stands in its ruthless way. It controls "fortune." But the peasant is not afraid.

*Edgar:* Good gentleman, go your gait, and let poor voke pass. An chud ha' bin zwaggered out of my life, 'twould not ha' bin zo long as 'tis by a vortnight. Nay, come not near th' old man. Keep out, che vore ye, or Ise try whether your costard or my ballow be the harder. Chill be plain with you.

*Oswald:* Out, dunghill!

*They fight.*

*Edgar:* Chill pick your teeth, zir. Come! No matter vor your foins.

[*Oswald falls.*]

*Oswald:* Slave, thou hast slain me.

Thus, once more the lowly good turns against the mighty evil—and defeats it. *Peasant, slave, villain, dunghill.* Cornwall and Oswald use the same language in the same situation. But the opposition to the evil has spread from the centre to the outskirts now. The country is more deeply involved now. The wooden staff defeats the steel sword. And note the scorn in the peasant's words—and the strength too. The convulsion is almost over, order is being restored, and it is basic humanity that is restoring it.

The device of the incriminating document is probably as old as literature itself. It represents a fortuitous accident that can suddenly manipulate, influence, or round out action. Its sudden emergence does not derive from the psychology or morality of the principals. Note that in *King Lear* Shakespeare utilizes his multifunctional character, Edgar, for the theatrical device of Goneril's letter in which she has indicated her and Edmund's criminal intentions.

At the first sight of Edgar in the play, Edmund said, "Pat! he comes, like the catastrophe of the old comedy. My cue is villainous melancholy, with a sigh like Tom o' Bedlam." Perhaps not one but two of Edgar's functional roles are foreshadowed in this curiously theatrical language. For, pat, he does come, the event which brings the Edmund success-story in *King Lear* to an end. When Edgar enters in the last scene

74

he is "armed," i.e., helmeted. No one on the stage knows who he is. This is his last disguise. He then defeats Edmund in trial-by-combat. We of the audience surmise *but do not know definitely* that this is Edgar. "I can produce a champion," he has told Albany. Do we not get the impression—before he reveals himself—that this unknown champion is not so much an individual as a personification of justice?

Are we to regard Banquo and Edgar as psychological unities, or are they primarily dramatic functions? I have tried to show that the plays themselves indicate they are the latter.

# 4

# Hamlet and Ophelia

Here I have set myself a problem, that of the relationship of the hero and Ophelia, in a notoriously debated play, *Hamlet.* What was really enlightening as I worked at the exercise was the irresistible recognition that the real answer to the problem was a full awareness of the problem itself, in all its evasive intricacy. Bradley wrote:

> Where he [the critic] remains in doubt he may say so, and, if the matter is of importance, he ought to say so.
>
> This is the position in which I find myself in regard to Hamlet's love for Ophelia. I am unable to arrive at a conviction as to the meaning of some of his words and deeds, and I question whether from the mere text of the play a sure interpretation of them can be drawn.[1]

But Bradley assumed that the original production had made matters clear. Because of the nature of the play itself, I do not believe that we can allow Bradley, or others, that assumption.

In 1.2 in which we are introduced to the Danish court, it

is important that Ophelia be present.[2] She says nothing, but she must, because of her father's position, be a conspicuous member of that glittering, acquiescent assemblage—which, again, must be in strong contrast to the solitary, black-costumed figure of the protagonist. Hamlet rejects *seems:* he stresses that in him there is correspondence between the inner and the outer man. But Claudius chides him, as though he were a schoolboy, in ready-to-hand, flowing, surface language. This style contrasts sharply with the almost inarticulate passion of the "O that this too too solid flesh would melt" soliloquy. The motif of this soliloquy is "Frailty, thy name is woman." The sudden shift in his mother's affection has disrupted Hamlet's concept of order to such an extent that he is suicidal. "All the uses of this world" are so nasty that he craves not so much death as oblivion. It is significant that the first person to whom he shows affection, Horatio, now enters, and that the latter has not been part of the King's retinue. Certainly, this entire scene declares that Hamlet is dissonant with the court and that broken faith among those to whom he is allied awakens a resonant reaction. So it is wise to remember the Hamlet of 1.2 while we are watching 1.3, in which we hear for the first time about his attentions to Ophelia.

Laertes is parting from his sister, and giving her advice about Hamlet. It is a family scene, in which the two are intimate and devoted. He plays the role of the elder brother, and she cheeks him. Yet one feels, obscurely, that both of these creatures lack substance. There is something counterfeit and tawdry about Laertes' language. It tends to bombastic indirection.

> For nature crescent does not grow alone
> In thews and bulk; but as this temple waxes,

The inward service of the mind and soul
Grows wide withal.

It is repetitive:

Then weigh what loss your honour may sustain
If with too credent ear you list his songs,
Or lose your heart, or your chaste treasure open. . . .

This is court language, which we have already had a taste of
from Claudius, and which we shall hear, fulsomely, in Polonius
and Osric; and in Laertes here, it hides, as always, shallowness
and corruption. The Hamlet whom we have just met could
not possibly be a seducer; nor would he easily listen to "the
main voice of Denmark." Moreover, Ophelia's buoyant raillery
not only suggests the possibility of her brother's future deprav-
ity but also, because it is not serious, her affinity to him.

What Ophelia tells her father later in the scene is the fullest
evidence we have in the play concerning the depth and dignity
of Hamlet's love for her—although, perhaps, it is necessary to
state that it is only Ophelia, herself, who gives us this information:

He hath, my lord, of late made many tenders
Of his affection to me.

My lord, he hath importun'd me with love
In honourable fashion.

And hath given countenance to his speech, my lord,
With almost all the holy vows of heaven.

There are fear and obedience in Ophelia's triple-repeated "my
lord." But Polonius, cynical and worldly, understands neither
her innocence nor Hamlet's; he besmirches and vulgarizes:

Affection? Puh!

79

> Tender yourself more dearly,
> Or (not to crack the wind of the poor phrase,
> Running it thus) you'll tender me a fool.

Ophelia is a "green girl." Hamlet is a rake whose offers are not "sterling," and whose vows are "pious bawds." Surely, as we remember the sensitive, idealistic, plain-speaking prince of 1.2, we conclude that Polonius' analysis of Hamlet is both cheap and erroneous. We particularly remember that Hamlet had taken himself out of the class of those who "seem." Here, with conventional and undiscriminating worldliness, Polonius puts him back into it.[3] To which side, her father's or her lover's, will Ophelia incline? The answer includes a fourth repetition of timid respect: "I shall obey, my lord." (What else should she do as a good daughter? Well, there is a long list: Desdemona, Jessica, Cordelia, Sylvia, etc.) And in separating from Hamlet at this momentous time she is allying herself, willy-nilly, with the court from which he is alienated.

Scene 4 is in biting cold outdoors, but we hear the warm, gay interior: "A flourish of trumpets, and two pieces go off." Claudius and the court are carousing: drink, dance, music. In this scene Shakespeare establishes further the contrast between the real Hamlet and the Laertes-Polonius Hamlet, between the almost puritanical prince and the hedonistic king, queen, and courtiers. Whereas in the second scene, Hamlet had indicated that a man must be pure to himself—"I know not seems"— here he stresses that a man must also appear pure to society. The Danes' habit of drinking "soils" their reputation; a single defect in "plausive manners" causes "scandal" in the "general censure." How glib, superficial, and mundane Polonius' famous advice to his son appears now in retrospect! But, if we shift our viewpoint, how arrogantly and destructively moralistic the protagonist, Hamlet, is!

So far we have seen a misanthropic, idealistic young man. He has violently rejected his mother and uncle and has been alienated from the court. Yet his emotions, as we look from those people to him, seem excessive. The Ghost provides an adequate cause for Hamlet's strong emotions. He now has an objective correlative. Beneath the "seems" his mother is not merely frail but "pernicious," his uncle not merely a satyr but a "villain." Thus, Hamlet has to set right the disjointed time. One of his modes in this endeavor, he tells us, will be a personal *strangeness, oddness,* "an antic disposition."

The Reynaldo-Polonius interview in 2.1 shows us again how spiritually corrupt these court creatures are. We see Polonius devising, with relish and pride, a scheme for spying on his own son. As he slighted the moral strength of his daughter, so now he has no faith in the moral strength of his son. But it is not, we discover, that he wants to tutor his son to live a sinless life; it is rather that he wants to know all about Laertes' actions abroad. He is curious, not morally zealous— and how thin his morality is! To Hamlet "one defect" could destroy a good man's whole reputation. To Polonius, "drinking, fencing, swearing, quarreling/Drabbing" are normal, youthful failings.[4] And if one is careful with one's words, immorality vanishes: "drabbing" is not "incontinency." So Shakespeare epitomizes this court figure as one who is worldly, cunning, incapable of noble faith and suspicious of noble resolves, one to whom honor is merely a matter of correct surfaces, a matter of "seems." But he is neither righteous nor cruel.

Hamlet is. From the eighteenth century to the present, from Johnson and Steevens to G. Wilson Knight and L. C. Knights, critics have pointed out Hamlet's brutality, occasionally or consistently, to Polonius, Gertrude, Claudius, Guildenstern and Rosencrantz, and Ophelia—especially to Ophelia.[5] Yet they

81

have been somewhat reluctant to stigmatize Hamlet as cruel in one particular episode which occurs off-stage, that in which the hero frightens Ophelia while she is sewing in her chamber. So difficult is this reported scene to construe that there are responsible interpreters who claim that it never really happened at all, that it was only an hallucination on Ophelia's part, a harbinger of her future insanity.[6] But granted that it did, indeed, take place, what are we to make of it? So far, in the play, we have only heard at second hand of Hamlet's attentions to the girl. We have not yet seen them together, to learn and understand with our own eyes and ears. Then Shakespeare deliberately presents us with a meeting of the two, but one which we are not allowed to witness, which we are compelled to decipher, and which we are not, there can be no gain-saying, given sufficient data to decipher. No wonder the critics disagree.

Ophelia rushes to her father to tell him what has just occurred. Disheveled, pale, his knees knocking together, with horrible suffering on his face, Hamlet had looked hard at her, sighed shatteringly, and walked out with his head twisted backwards. How are we to interpret Hamlet's actions here, broken heart or antic disposition? "This is no mock-madness," says G. Wilson Knight. "Hamlet would not first try the practical joke of pretended madness on Ophelia whom he loved. . . . The suggestion that in these circumstances, at this moment in his history, he has the presence of mind to pretend madness to Ophelia is, indeed, a perversion of commentary." [7] Boas is not so sure: "Hamlet, in his turmoil of soul, may be groping for latent sources of support in Ophelia's nature, but his method of inquisition seems deliberately arranged for the purpose of startling the timid girl out of her wits." [8] Neither is Bradley sure: "His *main* object in the visit appears to have been to convince *others,* through her, that his insanity was not due to any mysterious unknown cause, but to this disappointment [in love], and so allay the suspicions of the King." [9] Nor is Granville-Barker sure: "Is he [Hamlet] still as frenzied as we have ourselves seen him to be, or only pretending to be so, or partly pretending to be so and partly—? But what Shakespeare wants is just to this extent to puzzle us. . . ." [10]

Either Hamlet has been unmanned by Ophelia's rejection, or his confronting her is the first step in his antic disposition campaign against Claudius. At this particular moment, the audience can neither demand nor the play supply a choice of these alternatives. As Granville-Barker suggests, Shakespeare wants to puzzle us—and make us wait expectantly for the rest of the play to give us evidence for solving the puzzle. Nevertheless, we may surmise. On the one hand, when Hamlet's faith in Ophelia, almost a last hope (for whom else does he have to trust except Horatio?) is broken, he might actually lose control of himself. On the other hand, if Ophelia now fits into his earlier emotional conclusion, "Frailty, thy name is woman," a righteous Hamlet might make her, Ophelia, a symbol for all he despises and ruthlessly employ what he formerly loved against that of which he now believes her to be an unresisting part: Claudius and the court. Hamlet will later say of his former friends, Guildenstern and Rosencrantz,

> 'Tis dangerous when the baser nature comes
> Between the pass and fell incensed points
> Of mighty opposites.

Ophelia, to us, perhaps, is merely obedient to Polonius, her father, but, to Hamlet, she is obedient to Polonius, a completely and hence viciously representative court figure. However, Hamlet's using her as a pawn would indicate in him mental and emotional qualities which even those critics who stress his brutality and destructiveness would prefer not to name.

After Ophelia's recital, Polonius concludes that Hamlet's madness is "the very ecstasy of love" and leaves immediately to tell Claudius. In the next scene, 2.2, the latter informs us

> Of Hamlet's transformation. So I call it,
> Sith nor th' exterior nor the inward man
> Resembles that it was.

Note the sequence. At the end of the first act, Hamlet announces that "hereafter" he may "put an antic disposition on." In the first scene of the second act, we hear through Ophelia of Hamlet's acting for the first time *oddly* and *strangely*. Now at the beginning of 2.2, we discover that Hamlet's transformation is a matter of fact and knowledge to the Danish court. This sequence is part of the evidence we must struggle with in determining what the off-stage sewing-closet scene meant and means.

His mother failed him. Ophelia failed him. Now Guildenstern and Rosencrantz, his former close companions, will fail him. They have been summoned to discover what "unknown" afflicts the prince. Gertrude declares, "And sure I am two men there are not living/To whom he more adheres." Yet we see these "excellent good friends" acceding to the King's request to spy on Hamlet as easily as Reynaldo acceded to Polonius' to spy on Laertes. Ophelia prefers Polonius to Hamlet, Guildenstern and Rosencrantz prefer Claudius to Hamlet. The solitariness of the hero which we first noticed in 1.2 is being reinforced.

Later in 2.2, Shakespeare makes the answer to the Ophelia-Hamlet puzzle even more elusive. According to Polonius,

84

Ophelia's rejection was "the very cause of Hamlet's lunacy."
Then he reads a letter:

> To the celestial, and my soul's idol, the most beautified
> Ophelia. In her excellent white bosom, these, &c.
>
> > Doubt thou the stars are fire;
> > > Doubt that the sun doth move;
> > Doubt truth to be a liar;
> > > But never doubt I love.
>
> O dear Ophelia, I am ill at these numbers; I have not
> art to reckon my groans; but that I love thee best, O most
> best, believe it. Adieu.
> Thine evermore, most dear lady, whilst this machine
> is to him,
>
> > > > > Hamlet.

When was this letter written, before the rejection or afterwards? [11] If it was written afterwards, are we to consider it
sincere, or a deliberate device to mislead Ophelia, and hence
Polonius and Claudius? The play offers no definite answer.
But this is stumbling poetry, worse than Orlando's.[12] An
anonymous critic in 1736 declared the letter "too Comick for
this piece." [13] Indeed, it bears the mark of the Osric style[14]—
although the play later on shows Hamlet totally opposed to this
style, shows him as a discriminating student of verbal art, and
offers us two letters by him in 4.6 and 4.7 that are far different
from this strange epistle to Ophelia. Now if this letter be a red
herring, how Hamlet must despise both the court literary taste
and the court acumen that could conceive of him as sincerely
writing such a composition! The King is not certain that love
for Ophelia was the cause of his nephew's madness: "Do you
think 'tis this?" "How may we try it further?" Hence, Polonius devises the plan for Claudius and himself to be hidden
while they watch Ophelia confront Hamlet.

Then the "poor wretch" enters reading, and the confident Polonius attempts to "board him." But the tables are turned. The antic Hamlet we ourselves actually see for the first time since his intention to be odd and strange is confident and cruel, playing with his victim. He calls Polonius a "fishmonger."

*Hamlet:* For if the sun breed maggots in a dead dog, being a god kissing carrion—Have you a daughter?
*Polonius:* I have, my lord.
*Hamlet:* Let her not walk i' th' sun. Conception is a blessing, but not as your daughter may conceive. Friend, look to't.

The "still harping on my daughter" convinces Polonious that his diagnosis of love-madness has been correct, but he does not understand the term, "fishmonger." We should. A fishmonger is a bawd, one who employs a prostitute for his business.[15] Hamlet is obliquely telling the old councillor that he is using his own daughter for evil ends. Let him watch out. The sun is the court, the place of the king. (Cf. "I am too much i' th' sun.") If Ophelia trusts to the court, she will be wholly corrupted. Thus Hamlet illustrates the stupidity of Polonius, who does not trust what Hamlet stood for but does trust what Claudius stands for! At any rate, Hamlet feeds Polonius' suspicions on the cause of his lunacy, but his past and present emotions concerning Ophelia are by no means clear.

After Polonius leaves, Hamlet discovers that his sworn friends, Guildenstern and Rosencrantz, are also completely untrustworthy. They let him down as badly as Ophelia has. There is control and strength in his reaction: he will "have an eye" of them. And he tells them in general but not in particular what is troubling him. Hamlet concludes, "Man delights not me—nor woman neither, though by your smiling you seem to say so." Does this mean: "Do not believe that I am in a lover's despair because of Ophelia?" And, again, we do not know the real thought behind the implied question. When Polonius re-enters, Hamlet again attacks him. The irony of calling Polonius "Jepthah," who sacrificed his own daughter because he promised foolishly, is clear. But perhaps there is even more cruel irony.

*Polonius:* If you call me Jepthah, my lord, I have a daughter
  I love passing well.
*Hamlet:* Nay, that follows not.
*Polonius:* What follows then, my lord?
*Hamlet:* Why, "As by lot, God wot. . . ."

Is Hamlet saying that he does not at all agree that Polonius, being what he is, *is* capable of truly loving his own flesh and blood? Nevertheless, again Hamlet is misleading Polonius about the cause of his lunacy, and again he is obliquely saying what he really thinks of Polonius' care of his daughter. But neither Hamlet's past nor present feelings toward the girl herself are clear. We can or cannot make something of the fact that she is not mentioned in the "O, what a rogue and peasant slave am I" soliloquy. We are more anxious than ever to witness their first on-stage meeting.

It occurs in 3.1. But first, in a few quick lines, Shakespeare exemplifies the Danish court. When Claudius calls Polonius and himself "lawful espials," we remember the parental instructions to Reynaldo. Ophelia is a submissive decoy. Gertrude, superficial and sanguine, hopes that Ophelia's "good beauties" are the "happy cause" of Hamlet's state and that Ophelia's "virtues" will bring him back to his "wonted way" to both their "honors." When Ophelia replies, "Madam, I wish it may," she is thinking of marriage and appears wholly unaware that, by doing what others have told her to do, she is betraying Hamlet for the second time! Polonius babbles pieties which ironically invoke judgment on himself: "with devotions visage . . . we do sugar o'er/The devil himself." Claudius, in an aside, reveals the ugly contrast between his "most painted word" and his past "deed," and, significantly, he uses the image of "The harlot's cheek, beautied with plast'ring art." So here we see the central persons of the court: A shallow queen. A hypocritical king, who is a fratricide. A bumbling old councillor, who uses his own daughter to trap the Prince. And Ophelia? Surely, her good beauties will be like the harlot's cheek; she will wear devotion's visage but her words will be painted. Critics have wondered why Hamlet explodes at her. Can he not read her and the court as well as we can?

The "To be or not to be" soliloquy is less personal than the earlier "O that this too too solid flesh would melt," but it has the same refrain: death is preferable to "the thousand natural shocks" of daily life, one of which is "the pangs of despis'd love." Only, of course, Hamlet means that they are not "natural" to him. The whole soliloquy is evidence of Hamlet's persistent tendency to make universals out of particulars, to treat a particular as though it were a universal. (This is the basis for his famous speech to Guildenstern and Rosencrantz in 2.2 on the world as a "sterile promontory" and for his soliloquy in 1.2 on the world as "an unweeded garden.") Now, after his soliloquy, when Hamlet sees Ophelia, he may not see Ophelia the individual so much as Ophelia the symbol of everything in life that pains him.

But the spectator does not see a symbol, he sees Ophelia, and he is not sharing Hamlet's consciousness but attempting to interpret it. Here is the scene which should resolve our confusion concerning the Prince's real feelings for the girl, but it certainly does not resolve this confusion. One has only to turn to Professor Sprague's *Shakespeare and the Actors, The Stage Business in His Plays* (1660-1905) to discover that directors and actors have felt the scene's difficulties and have attempted to resolve them in various ways *not warranted by the bare text itself*.[16] Does Hamlet see the hidden spies? Is he, therefore, addressing them instead of the girl? Or are we dealing with an auditory palimpsest in which something is meant for her and something for them? Or is everything meant for her and yet for them too? Does he make any gestures—slight, broad, or equivocal—that he still loves her, that he is disgusted with her, that he is torn between love and disgust, or that he is now indifferent to her personally but harshly using her as a weapon? We cannot answer these questions which any conscientious critic or truly interested spectator rightly considers he must answer. All that we can do is hear or read the words and go whither they obscurely send us.

His first words to her, "Nymph, in thy orisons/Be all my sins remember'd," are equivocal. Is *nymph* a cant word for prostitute? Does he merely mean *virgin, maiden?* If the latter, is he being sardonic? Should she pray for him because she is pure and he is not? Should she pray for him because she, as woman, has caused his impurity? One does not know. . . . When Ophelia says she has gifts to return to him, he denies he gave them. Then, in gentle, formal discourse, reminding him of his former sweet words, she offers the gifts again: "Rich gifts wax poor when givers prove unkind." Here she is, a tool for her father and king, talking as though there has merely been a lover's quarrel, the responsibility for which has been Hamlet's! No wonder Hamlet turns on her, asking whether she is "honest." She has become the type of faithless woman. She is not personal to him but ideological. What he says to her had its origin in disgust with his mother. "The time gives

89

it proof" that "beauty" will inevitably change chastity to a "bawd." And is not what Ophelia is doing here a conspicuous illustration of the "harlot's cheek"? The dishonesty (unchasteness) of Gertrude merges with the dishonesty (disloyalty, hypocrisy) of Ophelia. To us, the maiden herself is a pathetic dupe; to Hamlet, she is an instrument who is trying to make him a dupe.

*Hamlet:* I did love you once.
*Ophelia:* Indeed, my lord, you made me believe so.
*Hamlet:* You should not have believ'd me; for virtue cannot so inoculate our old stock but we shall relish of it.

Mankind is so depraved that any kind of virtue is almost impossible to it. Poor Ophelia thinks she alone is being rejected. No, it is all humanity that Hamlet is rejecting: "Get thee to a nunnery! Why would'st thou be a breeder of sinners. . . . We are arrant knaves all." Then he shows his prescience—and gives a warning. "Where's your father?" She lies: "At home, my lord." He warns: "Let the doors be shut upon him, that he may play the fool nowhere but in's own house." Again, he returns to one of his leitmotifs in the play—sexual impurity. No woman can be chaste. "Wise men know well enough what monsters you make of them." This is what woman is, Ophelia as well as Gertrude. All women are basically whores:

> Go to, I'll no more on't! it hath made me mad. I say, we will have no more marriages. Those that are married already—all but one—shall live; the rest keep as they are. To a nunnery, go.

Hatred for Claudius and Gertrude erupts over poor Ophelia. But her simplicity and weakness, in the situation, are a kind of corruption too. Her "ignorance" in the circumstances is "wantonness."

90

Shakespeare stresses this, I think, in her speech after Hamlet leaves:

*Ophelia:* O, what a noble mind is there o'erthrown!
   The courtier's, scholar's, soldier's, eye, tongue, sword,
   Th' expectancy and rose of the fair state,
   The glass of fashion and the mould of form,
   Th' observ'd of all observers—quite, quite down!
   And I, of ladies most deject and wretched,
   That suck'd the honey of his music vows,
   Now see that noble and most sovereign reason,
   Like sweet bells jangled, out of tune and harsh;
   That unmatch'd form and feature of blown youth
   Blasted with ecstasy. O, woe is me
   T' have seen what I have seen, see what I see!

Contrast the stiff rhetoric of this passage—all surface and starch—with Hamlet's just concluded passionate discourse. Ophelia is beautiful and young—but there is no depth in her at all. A creature who, on such an occasion, could use the trope, "the courtier's, scholar's, soldier's, eye, tongue, sword," is pitifully incompetent in the Hamlet spiritual milieu. She thinks Hamlet insane. She hasn't even understood him. Claudius has:

   Nor what he spake, though it lack'd form a little,
   Was not like madness.

And Polonius and Claudius disregard her for the rest of the scene. There is a modicum of disgust in our feeling of pathos for her. "The little childish traitor!" says Miss Sitwell.[17] "[Cressida's] nearest sister is perhaps the pitiful and frail Ophelia," says E. K. Chambers.[18]

   In 3.2 the contrast between Hamlet's attitudes toward the faithful Horatio and the faithless Ophelia is pronounced. Hamlet's soul has chosen Horatio for its mate:

91

Since my dear soul was mistress of her choice
And could of men distinguish, her election
Hath seal'd thee for herself.

At the play-scene he is wantonly indecorous to the defenceless girl. That he wants to besmirch and hurt her seems obvious.[19] But is he again by his attentions to her both covering up his excitement and attempting to mislead, for the nonce, the King, and the rest? Polonius whispers to Claudius, "O, ho! do you mark that?" And surely Hamlet employs his "wildness" to tell the court (he is not whispering to Ophelia, is he?) what they really are beneath their painted faces and painted words. His mother is cheerful "and my father died within's two hours." Concerning the prologue, Ophelia says, " 'Tis brief." Hamlet replies, "As woman's love." Then,

*Ophelia:* You are as good as a chorus, my lord.
*Hamlet:* I could interpret between you and your love, if
    I could see the puppets dallying.
*Ophelia:* You are keen, my lord, you are keen.
*Hamlet:* It would cost you a groaning to take off my edge.
*Ophelia:* Still better, and worse.
*Hamlet:* So you must take your husbands.

Obliquely, Hamlet is calling Ophelia a puppet manipulated by others. That is why "your love" is not Hamlet: she has been faithless to Hamlet. And he warns her, as he had warned her father through her, that meddling in his plans is dangerous. Lastly, his reference to the marriage service scorns her leaving at a crucial time.

The scene with his mother in 3.4 reiterates the Hamlet whom we have already observed in his relationship with Ophelia. He lacerates Gertrude unmercifully about her infidelity. He dwells nauseatingly on her physical relations with Claudius. If she reveals to the King that Hamlet is really "mad in craft," she will "break [her] own neck down." Since he is "virtue itself" and the "scourge and minister" of Heaven, anything that stands in his way must obviously be brushed aside. The dead Polonius was a "rash intruding fool," "a foolish prating knave." There is gusto and relish in his brutality. And there is one particular speech which warrants our assumptions that Hamlet's reactions to his mother colored his reactions to Ophelia, that the one particular of his mother poisoned the whole universal of woman for him.

> Such an act
> That blurs the grace and blush of modesty;
> Calls virtue hypocrite; takes off the rose
> From the fair forehead of an innocent love,
> And sets a blister there; makes marriage vows
> As false as dicers' oaths. O, such a deed
> As from the body of contraction plucks
> The very soul, and sweet religion makes
> A rhapsody of words! Heaven's face doth glow;
> Yea, this solidity and compound mass,
> With tristful visage, as against the doom,
> Is thought-sick at the act.

And one may, also, think of Hamlet in regard to Ophelia as he sadistically describes to his mother his present feeling toward two others who also have been unfaithful to him:

> There's letters seal'd; and my two schoolfellows,
> Whom I will trust as I will adders fang'd,
> They bear the mandate; they must sweep my way
> And marshal me to knavery. Let it work;
> For 'tis the sport to have the enginer
> Hoist with his own petar; and 't shall go hard
> But I will delve one yard below their mines
> And blow them at the moon. O, 'tis most sweet
> When in one line two crafts directly meet.

93

There is an interesting confirmation of Hamlet's psychological habit of merging particulars in a class, as though each stood for all, in his farewell to the King in 4.3:

*Hamlet:* Farewell, dear mother.
*King:* Thy loving father, Hamlet.
*Hamlet:* My mother! Father and mother is man and wife; man and wife is one flesh; and so, my mother. Come, for England!

Unlike Hamlet's controlled, sharp "wildness," Ophelia's insanity in 4.5 is rudderless. Interwoven with the lost love of her dead father is the lost love of Hamlet. She has lost both now. Her "truelove," Hamlet, is out of the land; hence his dress of the pilgrim, cockle-hat and staff. "They say the owl was a baker's daughter." Because the baker's daughter was uncharitable to the Savior, she was turned into an owl. Perhaps here Ophelia is revealing ambiguously her feeling of guilt. Her Saint Valentine song concerns a lover rejecting his lady:

> Quoth she, 'Before you tumbled me,
> You promis'd me to wed.'

He answers—

> So would I 'a' done, by yonder sun,
> And thou hadst not come to my bed.

The lover rejects the lady because she has not remained pure. So Hamlet, when Polonius and Claudius were spying behind the arras, had seen through her harlot's countenance and treated her like a harlot. Thus, it may be not only her father's death but also grief and guilt over Hamlet that have cracked Ophelia's mind. When she enters again, Laertes greets her with rant:

> O heat, dry up my brains! Tears seven times salt
> Burn out the sense and virtue of mine eye!

94

And in her madness there is reference to a daughter. "It is the false steward, that stole his master's daughter." Polonius was a false steward who deprived his prince of his daughter. Then, Ophelia may possibly in flower language show us obliquely that she too has grasped the corruption of the King, the Queen —and herself. Fennel (flattery and deceit) to Claudius. Bitter rue (repentance) to Gertrude and herself—but Gertrude's repentance is to be "different" from Ophelia's! The daisy (dissembling in love) may be for all three of them—even for the absent Hamlet. Violets (faithfulness) are for none of them.

> And will he not come again?
> And will he not come again?
> No, no, he is dead;
> Go to thy deathbed;
> He will never come again.

Neither Hamlet nor her father will ever come again to her. She rejected one at the behest of the other, and now has lost both.

The shadow of the dead Ophelia is over all of 5.1. Until the funeral procession enters, Hamlet does not know that the gravedigger is working in her grave. There is no thought of her when he says to Yorick's skull, "Now get you to my lady's chamber, and tell her, let her paint an inch thick, to this favor she must come." But we may recall "painted word" and "harlot's cheek" and the ensuing meeting of the girl and Hamlet.

*Second Clown:* Will you ha' the truth an't? If this had not been a gentlewoman, she should have been buried out o' Christian burial.

*First Clown:* Why, there thou say'st! And the more pity that great folk should have count'nance in this world to drown or hang themselves more than their even-Christen.

95

(The priest later confirms the gravediggers' suspicion:

> And but that great command o'ersways the order,
> She should in ground unsanctified have lodg'd
> Till the last trumpet.)

Poor Ophelia. Doubtful in death as in life. And, again, the voice of the court has decided matters for her. Hamlet's macabre imagination converts the skulls into creatures that were once of the court: a circumventing politician, a sychophantic courtier, my Lady Worm, an avaricious lawyer. The "noble dust of Alexander" stops a bunghole, and that of Caesar patches a wall. To this ignoble end will come the schemes, the braveries of Claudius' entourage.

Then the funeral procession enters. The feckless Queen is still uncognizant as she scatters flowers:

> I hop'd thou should'st have been my Hamlet's wife;
> I thought thy bride-bed to have deck'd, sweet maid,
> And not have strew'd thy grave.

(We may recall other flowers.) Laertes rants. Hamlet comes forward, imitating Laertes' fustian:

> What is he whose grief
> Bears such an emphasis? whose phrase of sorrow
> Conjures the wand'ring stars, and makes them stand
> Like wonder-wounded hearers: This is I,
> Hamlet the Dane.

Laertes leaps at him, they grapple, and are parted. Then comes the final crucial passage in the play concerning the depth and reality of Hamlet's feeling for Ophelia. Each spectator or reader will extract from it exactly the information he requires to settle the matter.

*Hamlet:* Why, I will fight with him upon this theme
Until my eyelids will no longer wag.

*Queen:* O my son, what theme?
*Hamlet:* I lov'd Ophelia. Forty thousand brothers
  Could not (with all their quantity of love)
  Make up my sum. What wilt thou do for her?
*King:* O, he is mad, Laertes.
*Queen:* For love of God, forbear him!
*Hamlet:* 'Swounds, show me what thou't do.
  Woo't weep? woo't fight? woo't fast? woo't tear thyself?
  Woo't drink up esill? eat a crocodile?
  I'll do't. Dost thou come here to whine?
  To outface me with leaping in her grave?
  Be buried quick with her, and so will I.
  And if thou prate of mountains, let them throw
  Millions of acres on us, till our ground,
  Singeing his pate against the burning zone,
  Make Ossa like a wart! Nay, an thou'lt mouth,
  I'll rant as well as thou.
*Queen:* This is mere madness. . . .

Is this true grief for Ophelia? There is not a mention of her by Hamlet in the next and last scene of the play. How much does the love of "forty thousand brothers" weigh in the scales of reality?—As much as "Millions of acres"? Hamlet's numbers are not always to be trusted. In the "How all occasions do inform against me" soliloquy, Hamlet in his excitement converted "Two thousand souls and twenty thousand ducats" into "The imminent death of twenty thousand men" (4.4.25,60). Is not Hamlet but imitating Laertes' hyperbole?

    I have attempted some tentative answers in this paper concerning the Hamlet-Ophelia relationship. But they have had to be wrested from the play. And some, perhaps many, readers will throw these answers aside as forced or unnecessarily complex. The play itself gives no clear answers. That, I think, is the ultimate answer for *Hamlet,* that it should raise questions but never give forthright answers. It is oblique or vague or ambiguous where we want it to be blunt. In a kind of despair, Robert Bridges concluded that it was Shakespeare's deliberate design in *Hamlet* to "mystify" his audience. And, probably thinking of the hosts of warring commentators, Bridges added, ". . . does not the hypothesis of such a design reconcile all?" [20] I suggest that it not only, perforce, reconciles the critics but reveals, perhaps, the secret of the play's infinite attractiveness.

# 5

# *Shakespeare's Cleopatra*

*M*y purpose here is to indicate the essential unity of
Shakespeare's Cleopatra. It probably says nothing which has
not in general statements already been suggested by other
critics. But it does bring into sharper focus a salient quality in
her character which commentators have tended to shy from.
One either reads the play or he does not read the play. The
critic, as well as the editor, cannot, by his very vocation, be a
Bowdler. Furthermore, I definitely violate one of the standards
of the kind of dramatic criticism in which I believe; I separate
a character from the play in which this character is but one seg-
ment of the plot. In art the whole is greater than the sum of its
parts. Cleopatra does not exist in the artifact apart from
Antony, Iras, and the rest. It is the interaction of the deeds,
speeches, and personalities of all the characters that makes up
a play. The audience sees not a single figure but an ensemble,
hears not a solo but a symphony. I have tried to show my
awareness of this fact in some of my notes.

Schücking asserts that Cleopatra is not a unified, coherent, consistent character. The woman of the last two acts, "inwardly and outwardly a queen, has but little in common with the harlot of the first part." [1] Before Antony's decline she is a strumpet;[2] in the last events she is "an ideal figure," comparable to Desdemona and Imogen.[3] Herford refuses to accept Schücking's analysis:

> We are here concerned only to describe a critical method, not to discuss its results; but it is obvious to note, first, that the drama describes precisely a growth of the light liaison between the triumvir and the queen into a fierce though fitful passion which has moments of self-forgetting devotion (when no serious sacrifice is involved); and second, that even in this second phase the coquette, even the hard and brutal woman, flashes out at moments too; in her consummate dying speech, lover and actress, the jealous woman and the magnificent queen, the mistress of a Roman, who wishes to die like him "after the high Roman fashion," and the Oriental weakling who experimented first in "easy ways to die"—all are intermingled. The test of Cleopatra's coherence is not that a rather wooden mind may not discover inconsistency in the play of her "infinite variety," but that she impresses our imagination, not in spite of her variety but by and through it, as a personality superbly real and one.[4]

Stoll sides with Herford:

> But the essential unifying element in the character is, I think, overlooked by both critics. It is . . . rather in the speech, the identity of tone, than in the deeper psychological structure or the mental attitude. It would take many words for me to show this—there are so many facets to her glittering figure—if indeed I could show it at all. There are glimpses of her humour, for instance, not only in her

100

death scene but at Antony's death. And her spontaneous explosiveness appears when she calls Dolabella a liar and vents her rage on Seleucus, as when she called Antony one, raved against the Messenger, and threatened Charmian with bloody teeth. She is not wholly sublime and ideal as Professor Schücking takes her now to be. She abuses the gods and rails at Fortune when Antony dies, as she has always done at whatever thwarted her. She remembers Octavia continually and vindictively, with her modest eyes and her dulness. But above all she keeps her vivacious manner when excited. "Note him," she had said in the first Act to Charmian; "Note him, good Charmian, 'tis the man; but note him." Again and again this dancing repetition recurs, as after Antony's death:

> What, what! good cheer! Why how now, Charmian,
> My noble girls! Ah women, women, look,
> Our lamp is spent.

> He words me, girls, he words me, that I should not
> Be noble to myself.

And how from beginning to end, through all her fits and starts, she keeps her languorous, voluptuous manner—

> Give me some music, moody food
> Of us that trade in love—

I need not undertake to show.[5]

Certainly, Schücking creates a false dichotomy. The queen who, in order to get herself back in her lover's esteem, sends Mardian to the grief-struck Antony to report that she has killed herself,—

> Say, that the last I spoke was "Antony,"
> And word it, prithee, piteously: hence, Mardian,
> And bring me how he takes my death (4.13.8-10)[6]—

is no Desdemona-like figure but one still capable of feminine wiles. The Cleopatra who in 5.2 lies to Caesar about her treasure and flies at the unfaithful Seleucus like an angry fishwife reminds us not of Imogen but of the Cleopatra who berated and mistreated the Messenger in 2.5. How much of the courtesan there is in that last jibe at the eunuch!

> Wert thou a man,
> Thou would'st have mercy on me. (5.2.173-4)

She had brutally taunted Mardian thus in 1.5.8-18. Nor is it amiss to point out that her suicide is no *purely* altruistic art. Of course, Shakespeare has made the death motives of his dazzling, many-hued queen complex. Of course, her love for Antony is a great cause. Still, Shakespeare does present as the most prominent of the motives for her last action a great fear of being an object in Caesar's triumphal march in Rome and of being the recipient of Octavia's "demuring." [7] Clearly Cleopatra is not in the last two acts what Schücking says she is— "all tenderness, all passionate devotion, all genuine, unselfish love." [8]

Despite the fault of apocalyptic interpretation which they share with the rest of G. Wilson Knight's work, certain pages in *The Imperial Theme*[9] demolish Schücking's position. Knight's running analysis of Cleopatra as she appears from beginning to end of the play stresses her essential unity. His study demonstrates that the "serpent of old Nile" does not cast her original skin. But not even Knight seems to recognize how basically the harlot she is. Furthermore, I think it worthwhile to point out that Shakespeare, besides using more obvious means to convey an impression of her unity, has subtly— but effectively—employed a device of speech decorum which does adumbrate a unified psychology in Cleopatra. It is something more important than what Stoll calls "identity of tone." It is the device of iterative imagery.[10] I hope to show that the

obvious harlot and the queenly lover both draw their meta-
phors from the same storehouse—or bagnio.

But before I come to Cleopatra herself, I would like to
point out shortly how she appears to others. Now, any excur-
sion into symbolism will set some readers' critical teeth on
edge. Let us therefore listen to the characters themselves.[11] First
hear Antony in Rome (3.4.22-3):

> If I lose mine honour,
> I lose myself.

In 1.4.55-71, we hear Caesar:

> Antony,
> Leave thy lascivious wassails. When thou once
> Was beaten from Modena, where thou slew'st
> Hirsius and Pansa, consuls, at thy heel
> Did famine follow; whom thou fought'st against,
> Though daintily brought up, with patience more
> Than savages could suffer: thou didst drink
> The stale of horses, and the gilded puddle
> Which beasts would cough at: thy palate then did deign
> The roughest berry on the rudest hedge;
> Yea, like the stag, when snow the pasture sheets,
> The barks of trees thou browsed'st. On the Alps
> It is reported thou didst eat strange flesh,
> Which some did die to look on: and all this—
> It wounds thine honour that I speak it now—
> Was borne so like a soldier that thy cheek
> So much as lank'd not.

In the next scene but one, in 2.1.23-7, Pompey, invoking Cleopatra to hold Antony in Egypt with "witchcraft," "beauty,"
"lust," exclaims:

> Tie up the libertine in a field of feasts,
> Keep his brain fuming; Epicurean cooks
> Sharpen with cloyless sauce his appetite;

103

> That sleep and feeding may prorogue his honour
> Even till a Lethe'd dulness!

Honour is equated with Antony's abstinence in food. Dishonour is equated with Antony's luxuriousness in food. And precisely this note of gourmandism is what Shakespeare uses again and again to characterize Cleopatra in the speeches of others. So, to begin with, she characterizes herself (1.5.29-31):

> Broad-fronted Caesar,
> When thou wast here above the ground, I was
> A morsel for a monarch.

And Cleopatra again, in the same scene, referring to the same affair:

> My salad days,
> When I was green in judgment, cold in blood (73-4).

So Pompey speaks of her (2.1.11-3):

> Mark Antony
> In Egypt sits at dinner, and will make
> No wars without doors.

Thus Enobarbus conceives of her in her first meeting with Antony (2.2.229-30):

> And for his ordinary pays his heart
> For what his eyes eat only.

So, too, does Enobarbus again (2.2.240-2):

> Other women cloy
> The appetites they feed; but she makes hungry
> Where most she satisfies;

Employing the same image, Pompey laughs at Antony (2.6.60-5):

*Pompey:* We'll feast each other ere we part; and let's
Draw lots who shall begin.
*Antony:* That will I, Pompey.
*Pompey:* No Antony, take the lot; but, first
Or last, your fine Egyptian cookery
Shall have the fame. I have heard that Julius Caesar
Grew fat with feasting there.

And Enobarbus once more (2.6.119-22):

*Enobarbus:* . . . Octavia is of a holy, cold, and still conversation.
*Menas:* Who would not have his wife so?
*Enobarbus:* Not he that himself is not so; which is Mark Antony. He will to his Egyptian dish again.

And Antony in scorn (3.13.116-8):

I found you as a morsel cold upon
Dead Caesar's trencher; nay, you were a fragment
Of Cneius Pompey's. . .

But perhaps the most interesting occasion of the image is the last (5.2.270-4). It is as though Shakespeare does not want us to forget that even in her moment of greatest regality, even in her moment of transfiguration, Cleopatra is still but a species of sensory satisfaction:

*Cleopatra:* Will it eat me?
*Clown:* You must not think I am so simple but I know the divell himself will not eat a woman: I know that a woman is a dish for the gods, if the divell dress her not.

Our interest in these pages is on the Cleopatra of the second half of the play. We need not stress how Shakespeare deliberately creates a bordello atmosphere in the Egyptian court by means of 1.2. What we want to see is the hetaira psychology of the queen. She herself makes no concealment of her fundamental vocation:

> Give me some music; music, moody food
> Of us that trade in love. (2.5.1-2)

Or of her fundamental bias, in her plain words to Mardian:

> I take no pleasure
> In aught an eunuch has. (1.5.9-10)

She tends constantly to think and speak in suggestive and erotic terms. Only Schücking[12] of all the critics has seen the amazing eroticism of

> O happy horse, to bear the weight of Antony!
> Do bravely, horse! for wot'st thou whom thou movest?
> (1.5.21-2)

and the even more striking concealed imagery of her first words to the Messenger from Italy:

> Ram thou thy fruitful tidings in mine ears,
> That long time have been barren. (2.5.24-5)

The clue to her basic make-up is given by Enobarbus (who, as critics have noted, plays the part of chorus in the drama) at the very beginning, in 1.2.134-40:

> Under a compelling occasion let women die: it were pity to cast them away for nothing; though, between them and a great cause, they should be esteemed nothing. Cleopatra, catching but the least noise of this, dies instantly; I have seen her die twenty times upon far poorer moment: I do think there is mettle in death, which commits some loving act upon her, she hath such a celerity in dying.

It does not require ingenuity to see the clustered double entendres in this passage.[13] What is important for our present purpose is put sufficiently by Case: "Enobarbus pictures death as a vigorous lover to whom Cleopatra yields willingly." According to this blunt soldier, then, Cleopatra is erotic to the quick. And it is no accident on Shakespeare's part that in 5.2 she does meet death exactly as Enobarbus here describes her meeting death.[14] In her suicide, imagery, statement, attitude show still the same basic psychology. She is still, however transformed, the same courtesan—avid of love, impatient, jealous of rivals, quick-tempered, voluptuous, feline, thinking in sheerly female terms. Let us look at this scene.

Iras returns with the apparel which Cleopatra has just ordered (5.2.226-8):

> Show me, my women, like a queen: go fetch
> My best attires: I am again for Cydnus,
> To meet Mark Antony:

She will meet death, then, as a woman preparing for a prospective lover.[15] And thus her very denial, immediately after "I have nothing/Of woman in me" (237-8), reinforces how much the woman she has been, is, and will be even to the last.

Iras has brought in the robe and crown. Cleopatra asks for them (278). She has "immortal longings" (279). The word "longings"! She speaks in terms of satisfaction of desires and wants this satisfaction. No more shall wine "moist this lip" (280). How conscious she is of the kind of life she is leaving. We are reminded of Pompey's, "Salt Cleopatra, soften thy waned lip!" (2.1.21). She is impatient, "Yare, yare, good Iras; quick." (281). Is she impatient because she now imagines her lover, Antony, calling and rousing himself to praise her act (281-3)? [16] She hears Antony mock Caesar (283-5). A few lines later she, herself, will take satisfaction in mocking the latter. Then impatiently, "Husband, I come" (285). And immediately after disclaiming the "elements" of "baser life" (287-8), she again displays impatience in "So; have you done?" (288).

107

She kisses Iras and Charmian. The line, "Come then, and take the last warmth of my lips" (289), is typical and evocative. Iras dies. The latter's death is described (291-4) in imagery which only one who trades in love would employ:

> Have I the aspic in my lips? Dost fall?
> If thou and nature can so gently part,
> The stroke of death is as a lover's pinch,
> Which hurts, and is desired.[17]

Cleopatra images death just as Enobarbus images it for her in 1.2.134-40. Then, just as she has been jealous of Fulvia and Octavia, she displays jealousy of Iras, fearing that Iras will meet Antony before her (229-301):

> If she first meet the curlëd Antony,
> He'll make demand of her, and spend that kiss
> Which is my heaven to have.[18]

So applying the asp to her breast, she impatiently addresses it (303-4):

> Poor venomous fool,
> Be angry, and dispatch.

Then the scornful tongue (which stung Antony in 1.1 and 1.3) speaks of Caesar slightingly as less than a worm, as a stupid ass (304-6):

> O could'st thou speak,
> That I might hear thee call great Caesar ass
> Unpolicied!

Only Cleopatra, so inextinguishably a woman, could compare the asp's biting with herself nursing a baby and being lulled into sleep by the sensation (306-8):

> Peace, peace!
> Dost thou not see my baby at my breast,
> That sucks the nurse asleep? [19]

And dying becomes such a voluptuous experience[20] that she almost cannot contain herself. The caress of death and of Antony blend into one (309-310):

> As sweet as balm, as soft as air, as gentle,—
> O Antony!

Immediately after her death Shakespeare sums up in Charmian's words the impression he has been endeavouring to convey to us. In lines 313-4 Charmian seems to conceive of death as a kind of harem-keeper who has just received a noteworthy addition. The word she uses is not "queen"; it is "lass":

> Now boast thee, death, in thy possession lies
> A lass unparallel'd.

To Caesar, too, even in death, she is the courtesan (343-5):

> but she looks like sleep,
> As she would catch another Antony
> In her strong toil of grace.

What Schücking and Knight do not note enough is that Shakespeare never for a moment ceases to picture Antony and Cleopatra as voluptuaries. Shakespeare illustrates in this play that flesh can be transmuted just so far:

*Maecenas:* His [Antony's] taints and honours
  Waged equal with him.
*Agrippa:* A rarer spirit never
  Did steer humanity: but you, gods, will give us
  Some faults to make us men. (5.1.30-3)

We may apply to Cleopatra what she says of the rural clown (5.2.235-6):

> What poor an instrument
> May do a noble deed!

But she dazzles the eyes. And she almost escapes moral judgment—but not quite. How consistent Shakespeare is in his depiction of her! Thirteen lines before the end of the play we are informed that she had made endless experiments in "easy ways to die."

# 6

# Romeo, Character and Style

*M*y students frequently accuse Romeo of being fickle. Why else should he transfer so quickly and so painlessly his love from Rosaline, whom the spectator is never allowed to see, to Juliet? These students cannot perceive what surely would have been made obvious to the convention-minded Elizabethan audience, whose opinion was probably guided by the actor's art, that Romeo-*cum*-Rosaline is playing a part, whereas Romeo-*cum*-Juliet is truly enmeshed, body and soul, in his passion for Capulet's daughter. This is why Shakespeare does not discourage us from laughing at the first Romeo. The young man has learned his fashionable literary Petrarchan rôle extremely well, and acts it out thoroughly for the observation of his parents and friends.

In *As You Like It* 3.2. Rosalind describes the conventional lover's appearance and attitude: "a blue [i.e., dark-ringed] eye and sunken . . . an unquestionable [i.e., unquestioning, worshipping] spirit . . . everything about [him] demonstrat-

111

ing a careless desolation," oblivious of self in his love for the paragon.

Mercutio describes the conventional lover's language in 2.4:

*Benvolio:* Here comes Romeo, here comes Romeo.
*Mercutio:* . . . Now is he for the numbers that Petrarch flowed in. Laura to his lady was but a kitchen wench— Marry, she had a better love to berhyme her—Dido a dowdy, Cleopatra a gypsy, Helen and Hero hildings and harlots, Thisbe a gray eye or so, but not to the purpose.

It is Benvolio and Montague in the first scene who give a full description of Romeo's recent strange behavior, inexplicable to the father. Romeo keeps constantly to himself. He cannot sleep and, in the covert of the dark woods, sheds tears. When day comes, the heavy-hearted young man steals home, shuts his windows and locks daylight out. No one, says Montague, can discover what ails his son, he is "to himself so secret and so close." I think the average Elizabethan spectator was already far ahead of the parent, knowing what bothered the lad. No one can find out what ails the young man, but as soon as Benvolio asks, Romeo blurts out that it is love! (Shakespeare, surely, is asking us to chuckle, to take not seriously the young man's deep predicament.) The Petrarchan mode is heavy upon Romeo. He observes that there has been a fight:

Here's much to do with hate, but more with love.
Why, then, O brawling love, O loving hate!
O anything of nothing first create!
O heavy lightness, serious vanity!
Misshapen Chaos of well-seeming forms!
Feather of lead, bright smoke, cold fire, sick health!
Still-waking sleep, that is not what it is!
This love feel I, that feel no love in this.

112

That he really doesn't know what the quarrel was about but goes immediately into this rodomontade about love and hate underscores his essential unseriousness. O, how desolate he is! "Dost thou not laugh [at me]?" he asks Benvolio after the above outburst.

*Benvolio:* No, coz, I rather weep.
*Romeo:* Good heart, at what?
*Benvolio:* At thy good heart's oppression.
*Romeo:* Why, such is love's transgression.
   Griefs of mine own lie heavy in my breast,
   Which thou wilt propagate to have it pressed
   With more of thine. This love that thou hast shown
   Doth add more grief to too much of mine own.
   Love is a smoke made with the fume of sighs;
   Being purged, a fire sparkling in lovers' eyes;
   Being vexed, a sea nourished with loving tears.
   What is it else? A madness most discreet,
   A choking gall, and a preserving sweet.
   Farewell, my coz.
*Benvolio:* Soft, I will go along.
   And if you leave me so, you do me wrong.
*Romeo:* But I have lost myself. I am not here.
   This is not Romeo; he's some other where.

Here there is so much posturing grief, so much paradox, that the *persona* appears almost askew on the healthy-appearing youngster. And rhyme is often in Shakespeare the sign of artificiality. I myself see the real person, feeling real hunger, appearing suddenly among the fustian:

> Alas, that love, whose view is muffled still,
> Should without eyes see pathways to his will.
> Where shall we dine?

But perhaps I am being too subtle?

The love affair being conventional, the servant yearns from afar, is utterly desolated by his mistress' rejection:

*Benvolio:* Then she hath sworn that she will still live chaste?
*Romeo:* She hath, and in that sparing makes huge waste;
   For beauty, starved with her severity,
   Cuts beauty off from all posterity.
   She is too fair, too wise, wisely too fair,
   To merit bliss by making me despair.
   She hath forsworn to love, and in that vow
   Do I live dead that live to tell it now.
*Benvolio:* Be ruled by me. Forget to think of her.
*Romeo:* O teach me how I should forget to think.

The young man's desire seems hopeless.

There is another nice touch of the robust true Romeo behind the Petrarchan masquerade in 1.2, the next scene. When Benvolio says, "Take thou some new infection to thy eye,/And the rank poison of the old will die," Romeo cannot resist cracking, "Your plaintain leaf is excellent for that"—medicine for a bruise! Benvolio is non-plussed by the sudden remark, and Romeo goes into his act again:

*Benvolio:* For what, I pray thee?
*Romeo:* For your broken shin.
*Benvolio:* Why, Romeo, art thou mad?
*Romeo:* Not mad, but bound more than a madman is:
   Shut up in prison, kept without my food,
   Whipped and tormented and—Good-den, good fellow.

This sudden breaking off is another subtle indication of how skin-deep Romeo's passion for Rosaline really is.

His beloved is to be at the Capulet feast. Benvolio promises that comparison of her with the other ladies there will make "thee think thy swan a crow." Romeo responds with bombastic utterance, employing reference to the burning of heretics:

   When the devout religion of mine eye
   Maintains such falsehood, then turn tears to fires.
   And these who, often drowned, could never die,

Transparent heretics, be burnt for liars.
One fairer than my love! The all-seeing Sun
Ne'er saw her match since first the world begun.

Here is over-wrought statement indeed!

The maskers scene in which we first see Romeo with Mercutio, 1.4, in a way prepares us for what is to follow, for Mercutio's concept of love is down-to-earth, not vulgar necessarily except to prudes, but witty in its insistence on the physical accompaniment of passion. To Romeo's mischievous friend, love is obviously not a mere matter of jeweled words. Romeo, however, continues his part: "I have a soul of lead/So stakes me to the ground I cannot move." But, and this is his first *serious* speech, Romeo presages an ominous outcome to this night's happenings:

> My mind misgives
> Some consequence yet hanging in the stars
> Shall bitterly begin his fearful date
> With this night's revels, and expire the term
> Of a despisèd life closed in my breast
> By some vile forfeit of untimely death.
> But He that hath the steerage of my course
> Direct my sail. On, lusty gentlemen.

The contrast in language, mood, and depth with what he has said from the beginning of the play is remarkable. This is the very first extended utterance of the real Romeo behind the Rosaline *persona* and foreshadows the tragic creature of 3.5 ("Dry sorrow drinks our blood") and the anguished, desperate, but controlled victim of the last act ("Is it e'en so? Then I defy you stars!").

Now, how by language, can Shakespeare differentiate between the stylized love for Rosaline and the romantic love for Juliet? The answer already lies in the adjective, *stylized*.

It is not that Romeo's feeling for the second lady employs language which is not what we term hyperbolic and romantic. But the later style does not make paradox an end in itself, it does not posture, it is exaggerated but not fustian: it is *personalized,* not taking its imagery from a common stockpile of wear-worn meanings, attitudes, and expressions but from the non-restricted heart. Although it may be couplet or even sonnet, it does not smack of yardstick rhetorical parallelism. It always fits the occasion of true romantic passion and is in essence as different from the Rosaline utterance as day is from night. Again, this is *personalized* love, and that is why the hand clasp and the kiss during the sonnet in which Romeo and Juliet first speak is not the aethereal thing that mere reading might tend to make it:

*Romeo:* If I profane with my unworthiest hand
　This holy shrine, the gentle sin is this:
　My lips, two blushing pilgrims, ready stand
　To smooth that rough touch with a tender kiss.
*Juliet:* Good pilgrim, you do wrong your hand too much,
　Which mannerly devotion shows in this.
　For saints have hands that pilgrims' hands do touch,
　And palm to palm is holy palmer's kiss.
*Romeo:* Have not saints lips and holy palmers too?
*Juliet:* Ay, pilgrim, lips that they must use in prayer.
*Romeo:* O then, dear saint, let lips do what hands do:
　They pray: Grant thou, lest faith turn to despair.
*Juliet:* Saints do not move, though grant for prayers' sake.
*Romeo:* Then move not while my prayers' effect I take.
　(1.5.91-104)

Juliet's "You kiss by th' book" is amusing, for hitherto Romeo has indeed loved by the book.

As Romeo insists to Friar Lawrence 2.3.85 ff., one major difference in his present passion is "Her I love now/Doth

116

grace for grace and love for love allow;/The other did not so."
This is not a servant-mistress affair, with its ultimate roots in
Petrarch to Laura, its attitudes and modes frozen at length in
innumerable Elizabethan sonnets. Shakespeare attempts to
portray and succeeds in portraying a youthful, fresh, deep,
maturing mutual passion. And Mercutio's semi-pornographic
lines to the hidden Romeo in 2.1 serve to highlight if only by
contrast the purity of the bodily passion that will be consum-
mated only in the sacrament of marriage:

> I conjure thee by Rosaline's bright eyes,
> By her high forehead and her scarlet lip,
> By her fine foot, straight leg, and quivering thigh,
> And the demesnes that there adjacent lie,
> That in thy likeness thou appear to us.

Mercutio "jests at scars that never felt a wound." This is
the wound not of an assumed fashionable malaise because of
Rosaline but one which opens the heart truly to the beloved:

> It is my lady; O it is my love.
> O that she knew she were.
> She speaks, yet she says nothing. What of that?
> Her eye discourses; I will answer it.
> I am too bold; 'tis not to me she speaks.
> Two of the fairest stars in all the heaven,
> Having some business, do entreat her eyes
> To twinkle in their spheres till they return.
> What if her eyes were there, they in her head?
> The brightness of her cheek would shame those stars
> As daylight doth a lamp; her eye in heaven
> Would through the airy region stream so bright
> That birds would sing and think it were not night.
> See how she leans her cheek upon her hand!
> O that I were a glove upon that hand
> That I might touch that cheek.

In the passage I have just quoted, the blank verse, the extreme commonness of expression in the first five lines (the language for Rosaline was never easy and common), the sequence of simple expression followed by the "newness," that is, the spontaneous, unlabored eye and star hyperbole, *all* mark this as Romeo's new way of speaking for a new way of feeling. And note how superbly the speech ends in the last three lines, how beautifully a glove upon a hand serves him for the deep-desired intimacy his heart moves him to.

Some may still say that Shakespeare does not distinguish enough between Romeo's two kinds of expression. But Shakespeare *cannot* succeed for those who do not, to begin with, accept the concept of romantic love for the two hours' traffic of our stage. It follows that such readers cannot discriminate between conventional Petrarchan love and the truly romantic sort, which approaches our real experience, if only when we are very young.

118

# 7

## The Two Angelos

*N*ot even Mary Lascelles' *Shakespeare's Measure for Measure* (1953), which is an almost word-for-word perception and analysis of the play, handles, or for that matter even recognizes, the problem I intend to deal with now, that of two strikingly disparate characterizations of the same character.

That Shakespeare, for the sake of the whole, for the sake of the entire impression which he wants a play to make, for the sake of the particular impression which he wants a play to make at a particular moment, could introduce a new motive for a particular character's actions, even at a relatively late or very late stage of the drama's progress, is proved by the clear insertion of Hamlet's ambition in the last act of his play.[1] And that critics have noticed the phenomenon, whether they have brought good evidence to support their claims or not, is indicated by certain pages of L. L. Schücking's *Character Problems in Shakespeare,* wherein he attempts to substantiate his hypotheses that there are two Julius Caesars

119

and two Cleopatras out of which no unified character analysis in the Bradleyan manner can be extracted. The example of Angelo, however, is definitive. It is impossible to bring the two divergent portrayals together. And one must assume that Shakespeare's change of the well-known story because of which the sister's virtue is not sacrificed forced the shift in Angelo's character, which is so well concealed that—to my great astonishment!—not even perceptive auditors and critics have noticed it.

Up to his exit at the end of 2.4, Angelo is a character who might vie with Macbeth in the split between his compulsive desires and his conscience. Frightening he is, even sadistic—as is implied by his treatment of Claudio, his blunt assertiveness to the decent and human-hearted Provost, and his abrupt dismissal of Elbow's "criminals," hoping they will all be whipped—contrast this last with the understanding tolerance of his fellow magistrate, Escalus. But Angelo here in these scenes is by no means an ignoble figure. He may lack empathy, but his view of law and justice is not despicable. This is a difficult play; Shakespeare does everything he can to show that a harsh attitude toward concupiscence may exist in heaven but not on earth. And determination is even further muddled by the friar Duke's harshness towards Juliet for the same "sin" which he later encourages Mariana to commit and Isabella to aid.[2] Nevertheless, it would be impossible for an enlightened jurist to impugn Angelo's statements to Escalus or to Isabella. Let us look at some of these. Escalus says in 2.1:

> Ay, but yet
> Let us be keen and rather cut a little,
> Than fall and bruise to death. Alas, this gentleman
> Whom I would save had a most noble father.
> Let but your honor know,

120

Whom I believe to be most strait in virtue,
That in the working of your own affections,
Had time cohered with place or place with wishing,
Or that the resolute acting of your blood
Could have attained th' effect of your own purpose,
Whether you had not sometime in your life
Erred in this point which now you censure him,   ·
And pulled the law upon you.

To which Angelo replies:

'Tis one thing to be tempted, Escalus,
Another thing to fall. I not deny
The jury passing on the prisoner's life
May in the sworn twelve have a thief or two
Guiltier than him they try; what's open made to justice,
That justice seizes; what knows the laws
That thieves do pass on thieves? 'Tis very pregnant
The jewel that we find, we stoop and take't
Because we see it; but what we do not see
We tread upon, and never think of it.
You may not so extenuate his offense
For I have had such faults; but rather tell me,
When I that censure him do so offend,
Let mine own judgment pattern out my death
And nothing come in partial. Sir, he must die.

Angelo's speech not only defends the integrity of the law but
even admits the possible defalcation of the lawmaker and law
enforcer. This is great utterance, and there is nothing in the
least pernicious about it. Similarly, although our hearts go
out wholly to Isabella in mercy in 2.2, yet the Angelo who says

The law hath not been dead, though it hath slept.
Those many had not dared to do that evil
If that the first that did th' edict infringe
Had answered for his deed. Now 'tis awake,
Takes note of what is done, and like a prophet

> Looks in a glass that shows what future evils,
> Either new, or by remissness new-conceived,
> And so in progress to be hatched and born,
> Are now to have no successive degrees,
> But, ere they live, to end.

is a keen if hard protector of orderly society. We should remember that a merciful God is also an all-knowing One: man in his hopes and fears for the future must perforce be, fortunately or unfortunately, legalistic.

When and as Angelo falls, he falls as a great man. He is tempted not as a Lucio, to engage in momentary sport, but as a noble victim of a completely uncontrollable emotion. This is not lechery; this is the complement of the strong rigidity that has hitherto guided him. He like his counterparts Coriolanus, Othello, Lear, and Macbeth is swept on to irresponsibility by a force that in its strength shows that it is outside reason. The essence of the situation is magnificently phrased by Angelo himself when in an aside he states that he is "that way going to temptation/Where prayers cross." Consider the word *love* in the following soliloquy that ends 2.2:

> From thee: even from thy virtue.
> What's this? what's this? is this her fault or mine?
> The tempter, or the tempted, who sins most?
> Ha!
> Not she, nor doth she tempt; but it is I
> That, lying by the violet in the sun,
> Do as the carrion does, not as the flower,
> Corrupt with virtuous season. Can it be
> That modesty may more betray our sense
> Than woman's lightness? Having waste ground enough,
> Shall we desire to raze the sanctuary
> And pitch our evils there? O fie, fie, fie!
> What dost thou? or what art thou, Angelo?

Dost thou desire her foully for those things
That make her good? O, let her brother live:
Thieves for their robbery have authority
When judges steal themselves. What, do I love her,
That I desire to hear her speak again,
And feast upon her eyes? what is't I dream on?
O cunning enemy that, to catch a saint,
With saints dost bait thy hook: most dangerous
Is that temptation that doth goad us on
To sin in loving virtue. Never could the strumpet
With all her double vigor, art and nature,
Once stir my temper; but this virtuous maid
Subdues me quite. Ever till now,
When men were fond, I smiled and wondered how.

Angelo does not say merely that he lusts after Claudio's sistei;
he says that he *loves* her. The appetite here is the opposite of
momentary lust. It is the ruthless compulsion that makes of
Maugham's *Of Human Bondage* and even sometimes of the
cheapest opera an artifact that has disturbing credibility. This
is what drives Romeo and Juliet together.

Seized by this emotion Angelo confronts Isabella in 2.4.
His admissions are illuminating. "We are all frail," he says;
"Plainly conceive, I love you"; and again, your brother "shall
not [die], Isabel, if you give me love." (It is the sublimity of
Shakespeare's irony that not until this moment of intimate
non-intimacy do the two call each other by their names!) The
very beat and tautness of his lines show a ruthless but not small,
a savage but not cheap, villain:

Answer me tomorrow,
Or, by the affection that now guides me most,
I'll prove a tyrant to him. As for you,
Say what you can, my false o'erweighs your true.

After 2.4 Angelo makes no appearance until two full acts later, until 4.4, which is just upon the beginning of the last scene and act. Already as we know he is in the grip of the plot which will expose him. And the Angelo of the last scene is by no means the caught figure of Macbeth or Othello. He is there because he has to be the pawn of the theatricality that Shakespeare has invented. He has neither bulk nor credence. He is there to be exposed and then married and then freed. One might truly say that after 2.4 the great Angelo whom I have tried to describe in the first two acts has no part in the play. And I think one of the reasons why is not far to seek. Beginning with 3.1.204 the former Angelo disappears and a new Angelo replaces him:

*Duke:* . . . Have you not heard speak of Mariana, the sister of Frederick, the great soldier who miscarried at sea?

*Isabella:* I have heard of the lady, and good words went with her name.

*Duke:* She should this Angelo have married, was affianced by her oath, and the nuptial appointed: between which time of the contract and limit of the solemnity, her brother Frederick was wracked at sea, having in that perished vessel the dowry of his sister. But mark how heavily this befell to the poor gentlewoman: there she lost a noble and renowned brother, in his love toward her ever most kind and natural; with him the portion and sinew of her fortune, her marriage dowry; with both, her combinate husband, this well-seeming Angelo.

*Isabella:* Can this be so? Did Angelo so leave her?

*Duke:* Left her in her tears, and dried not one of them with his comfort; swallowed his vows whole, pretending in her discoveries of dishonor; in few, bestowed her on her own lamentation, which she yet wears for his sake; and he, a marble to her tears, is washed with them but relents not.

Let us hazard reasons why the second Angelo—small-minded, mean, calculating, vindictive—has to enter the play.

In order to get Isabella off the hook Shakespeare has to employ "the bed-trick." Somebody else must substitute for Isabella in the garden that night. Since the coming together of Mariana and Angelo has to be legally and religiously acceptable, the bed-trick has to be advised by a friar. This can only come about by having had Angelo break a betrothal contract. One cause for breaking the contract could have been Angelo's finding a new love. But although Shakespeare can add demeaning traits to the old Angelo, he cannot without peril totally contradict the old Angelo. Now one of the most marked characteristics of the former Angelo was his initial non-amorous nature. Thus the only recourse for Shakespeare was to have the Angelo-Mariana betrothal broken because Angelo did not get the dowry he expected. The motive, in other words, for the rupture was avarice. But there is nothing in the early Angelo that prepares us for this miserliness. Furthermore, although his refusing Mariana comfort goes along with the sadism which I have remarked, his pretence that Mariana was dishonorable is, I think, also denied by our impression of the original Angelo. That he would be thus cheap and mean does not seem possible. This avaricious and small-minded creature, a jilting Angelo, is a far cry from the noble, if too noble for his own good, character who inhabits the play in the first two acts.

When Angelo changes, the play changes. What has been hitherto almost a deterministic sequence of events between a man and a woman becomes a theatrical trickery the virtues of which I would not deny. Nevertheless these are easier virtues than those which possess the great tragedies, effective as they too are on the stage.

Hence I do not think I am wrong in assuming that the shift that most people feel in *Measure for Measure* from a great drama to a great theatrical and ideological drama is occasioned as much as anything by the fact of the two Angelos.

# 8

## Margaret, or Much Ado about Convention, Consistency, Psychology, and Reality

*Much Ado About Nothing* can be regarded almost as a lesson in how to receive certain of Shakespeare's characters. Resembling *As You Like It,* which, as Harold Jenkins has pointed out in a very fine essay (*Shakespeare Survey VIII*), is a parody of itself, *Much Ado* on occasion points almost ostentatiously at its pervasive unseriousness. In other words, to be critically sensitive to *Much Ado* requires that one be fully aware of its constant tongue-in-cheek approach to what it is setting forth. When Don John says in 1.3, "I cannot hide what I am. . . . I am a plain-dealing villain," he is warning the reader not to psychologize his motives—the reader, not the spectator, for the latter sitting in his seat, watching the performance, has a quick eye and ear for stock character and characterization. But not all the characters in this fine play belong to melodrama.

Hence it is that the audience quickly differentiate on the basis of simplified utterance, of recognition of what they have seen before in other plays, and possibly of revealing costume—such as an absolute white gown on the heroine—between Beatrice and Benedick on the one hand and Hero and Claudio on the other. The former are as mysterious and complex as people can be: the latter are well-known and immediately recognizable stock characters. Hero and Claudio are not psychologized by the author because to do so would render even more improbable the events in which they are concerned, the events for which they have been fashioned. These events are made as artificial as possible to fit the *novella* characters and *vice versa*. Shakespeare is at pains to emphasize the conventional nature of the plot in which his hero and heroine are disposed. He is at pains to make them the puppets of their action rather than its instigators.

But in the midst of his puppets and pasteboard, Shakespeare inserts Beatrice and Benedick, who possibly rival the main characters of the great tragedies in the emphasis Shakespeare puts upon them, in the space they occupy, and in the complexity of their psychologies. Thus, we cannot, as some critics do, go at the characters in an individual play as if they all came out of the same kind of mold. With Beatrice and Benedick Shakespeare claims not only that there can be imaginary toads in imaginary gardens but that there can be real toads among the artificial ones. The technique of *Much Ado* in regard to Beatrice and Benedick is much like that of Walt Disney when he places live actors or actresses in his cartoon world of imaginary creatures and fantastic events. The contrast between formally real and essentially unreal, between complexity and simplicity, between reality and convention, pervades *Much Ado*.

One can see what Shakespeare is up to in the very first scene

128

of the play. For the first 150 lines Claudio, the hero, says nothing, Hero, the heroine, in the entire scene speaks one line which has nothing to do with herself, and the villain says merely, "Thank you. I am not of many words, but I thank you." What need these stage creatures say? Hero and Claudio have only to look at each other to fall in love. Villain is established as villain by his curt manner and dark clothing. But note that in this same scene three-quarters of the utterances are given to Beatrice describing Benedick to the messenger *and* Beatrice and Benedick arguing with each other soon after Don Pedro and his retinue enter. Let us glance at Hero's fatuous one line. Beatrice has asked the Messenger whether Signior Mountanto has returned from the wars too. Hero interprets, "My cousin means Signior Benedick of Padua." In the play the hero and the heroine do talk, and sometimes a great deal, but until the great church scene of Act 4 and even after that, hero and heroine engage in extended talk only when what is being talked about does not concern them particularly and/ or concerns Beatrice and Benedick.

To sum up, the characters of the main plot are plot-ridden; the characters of the subplot have depth and width similar to real people. But all of Shakespeare's machination has not yet been disclosed. Just as Hero and Claudio tend to escape from convention in the presence of Beatrice and Benedick (i.e., when their own characters and lives are not in focus), so the latter are fooled by the most outrageous convention of overhearing, in the entirely improbable dual scenes where they hear what psychologically they have been waiting to hear, that their opposite is in love with them. But here convention serves reality deeply. For Beatrice and Benedick are as real as you and I. We know they are in love from the first we see of them. Why else should each talk so much to the other, be so interested in the other? It is a later scene, the second scene of the fifth act, which explains them most clearly:

*Benedick:* Thou and I are too wise to woo peaceably.
*Beatrice:* It appears not in this confession. There's not one wise among twenty that will praise himself.
*Benedick:* An old, an old instance, Beatrice, that lived in the time of good neighbors. If a man do not erect in this age his own tomb ere he dies, he shall live no longer in monument than the bell rings and the widow weeps.
*Beatrice:* And how long is that, think you?
*Benedick:* Question: why, an hour in clamor and a quarter in rheum. Therefore is it most expedient for the wise, if Don Worm (his conscience) find no impediment to the contrary, to be the trumpet of his own virtues, as I am to myself. So much for praising myself, who, I myself will bear witness, is praiseworthy.

Each, Beatrice and Benedick, is properly in love with himself. Being in love is being vulnerable. Each at first hides his vulnerability with the disguise of attack. Each is willing to admit love when there is no longer any danger of hurt, when the other will not merely not attack the ego but accede to it and cherish it.

Once the general principles I have been stating as operative in the play are observed, everything in *Much Ado* seems to fall easily into place. Consider Margaret. Why is she not present in the church scene where she could have untangled the confusion in ten words? The answer is not psychological, has nothing to do with character. The answer comes from Shakespeare's theatrical need. The reason why she is not there is that she cannot possibly be there if the play is to go on. Shakespeare here kicks both probability and improbability out the door—

130

and we do not even notice. Similarly there is absolutely no connection between the Margaret of the Borachio plot and the Margaret whom we see on the stage. We first hear of Margaret's infatuation for Borachio in 2.2:

*Borachio:* I think I told your lordship, a year since, how much I am in the favor of Margaret, the waiting gentlewoman to Hero.
*John:* I remember.
*Borachio:* I can, at any unseasonable instant of the night, appoint her to look out at her lady's chamber window.
*John:* What life is in that to be the death of this marriage?
*Borachio:* . . . Find me a meet hour to draw Don Pedro and the Count Claudio alone; tell them that you know that Hero loves me; intend a kind of zeal both to the Prince and Claudio (as in love of your brother's honor, who hath made this match and his friend's reputation, who is thus like to be cozened with the semblance of a maid) that you have discovered thus. They will scarcely believe this without trial; offer them instances, which shall bear no less likelihood than to see me at her chamber window, hear me call Margaret Hero, hear Margaret term me Claudio, and bring them to see this the very night before the intended wedding; for in the meantime I will so fashion the matter that Hero shall be absent and there shall appear such seeming truth of Hero's disloyalty that jealousy shall be called assurance and all the preparation overthrown.

Unless we consider Margaret a complete schizophrenic cretin, we had better not confuse this Margaret II with the Margaret I whom we saw dancing with and talking to Balthasar in the preceding scene. Margaret I is a lady-in-waiting to Hero, witty, bantering, and imitative of her superiors. Shakespeare deliberately confuses us by stressing the dissimilarity between the two Margarets *for after all there is only one nominal Margaret in the play!* In scene 3.3 in which the watch arrest Don John's henchmen, Borachio says:

> Know that I have tonight wooed Margaret, the Lady Hero's gentlewoman, by the name of Hero. She leans me out at her mistress' chamber window, bids me a thousand times good night. I tell this tale vildly; I should first tell thee how the Prince, Claudio, and my master, planted and placed and possessed by my master Don John, saw afar off in the orchard this amiable encounter.

*Conrade:* And thought they Margaret was Hero?

*Borachio:* Two of them did, the Prince and Claudio; but the devil my master knew she was Margaret; and partly by his oaths, which first possessed them, partly by the dark night, which did deceive them, but chiefly by my villany, which did confirm any slander that Don John had made, away went Claudio enraged; swore he would meet her, as he was appointed, next morning at the temple, and there before the whole congregation, shame her with what he saw o'ernight and send her home again without a husband.

In the very next scene, enter Hero, Margaret and Ursula, and Margaret engages in intimate conversation with Hero about —of all things—her wedding gown and teases Beatrice about her concealed love! Here is a bit of her discourse to Beatrice:

*Margaret:* . . . You may think perchance that I think you are in love; nay, by'r lady, I am not such a fool to think what I list, nor I list not to think what I can, nor indeed I cannot think, if I would think my heart out of thinking, that you are in love, or that you will be in love, or that you can be in love. Yet Benedick was such another and now is he become a man; he swore he would never marry, and yet now in despite of his heart he eats his meat without grudging; and how you may be converted I know not, but methinks you look with your eyes as other women do.

132

Surely this Margaret I has no relationship with the drunkard's minion, Margaret II. The divergence and yet ultimate identity of the two Margarets are comically stressed in 5.1. Borachio confesses to Claudio and Don Pedro

> how Don John your brother incensed me to slander the Lady Hero; how you were brought into the orchard and saw me court Margaret in Hero's garments; how you disgraced her when you should marry her.

Then Leonato enters with the truth, faces Borachio:

> This naughty man
> Shall face to face be brought to Margaret,
> Who I believe was packed in all this wrong,
> Hired to it by your brother.
> *Borachio:* No, by my soul, she was not;
> Nor knew not what she did when she spoke to me,
> But always hath been just and virtuous
> In anything that I do know by her.

Does this make any sense to anybody? Of course not. And Shakespeare underlines its irrationality by having Margaret enter in the very next scene with Benedick, a Margaret strangely uncomprehensive of the dirty plot in which she has been concerned, a gay and buoyant Margaret exchanging witticisms:

*Margaret:* Will you then write me a sonnet in praise of my beauty?

*Benedick:* In so high a style, Margaret, that no man living shall come over it, for in the most comely truth thou deservest it.

*Margaret:* To have no man come over me? Why, shall I always keep below stairs?

*Benedick:* Thy wit is as quick as the greyhound's mouth; it catches.

We finish with Borachio's Margaret in the first lines of 5.4:

*Friar:* Did I not tell you [Hero] was innocent?
*Leonato:* So are the Prince and Claudio, who accused her
Upon the error that you heard debated.
But Margaret was in some fault for this,
Although against her will, as it appears
In the true course of all the question.

And thus is Margaret II exculpated by this meaningless verbiage. Since she is innocent the obvious schism between her and Margaret I disappears.

Thus does Shakespeare deliberately muddle, confuse, bedevil the audience, and bring and not bring the two Margarets together. The absence of jointure is so blatant that Shakespeare does not even try a rational amalgamation. Instead he seems willfully to call attention to the discrepancy: to say, as it were, "much ado about nothing" to Shakespeare critics who like to see in every character consistency, psychology, and reality. Now we should be prepared to take the play for what it is, a demonstrably artificial construct which the reality of Beatrice and Benedick strangely inhabits on occasion. Much critical confusion should cease once the true nature of the play is exposed. Here are some critical problems that I believe can be solved.

1. The flat blank verse at the end of the first scene: It would not do for Shakespeare to have Claudio and Don Pedro in anything that concerns the main plot take on stature and depth through important weighted incisive verse like that of Beatrice and Benedick's rich prose. So the verse is functionally flat.

2. The overuse of the convention of overhearing: In 1.2 Antonio's man overhears the Prince saying that he loves Hero and that he will woo her. In the following scene, 1.3, Borachio

reports that he has overheard that the Prince is going to woo for Claudio. In the next scene, 2.1, Don John concludes that Don Pedro is wooing Hero for himself and informs Claudio so, to the latter's jealousy. Borachio too is overheard by the watch. Even the trick by which Pedro and Claudio are manoeuvered into mistaking Margaret for Hero is a trick of planned overhearing! And I shall speak in a moment of the overhearing scenes by which Beatrice and Benedick are trapped into revealing their love for each other. Truly the ostentatiously artificial convention of overhearing touches almost everyone in the play! Obviously, Shakespeare is calling attention to the contrived nature of his comedy by overstressing an extremely conventional device.

3. Why has Shakespeare taken his stock hero and made him jealous and suspicious of Don Pedro in 2.1?—So that the audience will be confused in 3.2 when Don John falsely accuses Hero to Claudio and Don Pedro. For we know or think we know that Claudio having already been jealous will fall prey to his inner suspicion. But what about Don Pedro? He also immediately believes. So Shakespeare turns the convention of the liar believed in upon itself and blows yea and nay with the same breath.

4. Having done everything he can to make Beatrice and Benedick stand out in a play in which they ostensibly do not fit by any normal critical standard, Shakespeare, as it were, thumbs his nose at us by having their reality succumb to a cheaper trick than appears elsewhere in the drama. They are caught too by overhearing, not by a reported or accidental one but by a deliberate trick of their friends, open in all its crudity on the stage before us.

5. Hero's inability to clear herself in the church scene: Having emphasized Hero's shadowiness and thinness in every-

thing that concerns her, Shakespeare has inevitably made a weak characterization become a weak character. She cannot because of what she is, of what Shakespeare has made her, defend herself strongly at all. It remains for Beatrice, the stronger character and thicker characterization, to become wrought up and to become angry, independent, and wholly rounded in the great "Kill Claudio!" passage.

6. The Friar's plan for concealing Hero as dead, lines 210-243 in 4.1, thirty lines devoted to completing a second argument, where instead of coming indeed to a second conclusion they return by a wordy devious route to the conclusion that they were supposed to augment! (The italics are mine.)

*Friar:* Marry, this well carried shall on her behalf
Change slander to remorse; that is some good.
*But not for that dream I on this strange course,*
*But on this travail look for greater birth.*
She dying, as it must be so maintain'd,
Upon the instant that she was accus'd,
Shall be lamented, pitied, and excus'd
Of every hearer; for it so falls out
That what we have we prize not to the worth
Whiles we enjoy it, but being lack'd and lost,
Why, then we rack the value; then we find
The virtue that possession would not show us
Whiles it was ours. So will it fare with Claudio.
When he shall hear she died upon his words,
Th' idea of her life shall sweetly creep
Into his study of imagination,
And every lovely organ of her life
Shall come apparell'd in more precious habit,
More moving-delicate and full of life,
Into the eye and prospect of his soul,
Than when she liv'd indeed. *Then shall he mourn,*
If ever love had interest in his liver,
*And wish he had not so accused her,*

136

No, though he thought his accusation true.
Let this be so, and doubt not but success
Will fashion the event in better shape
Than I can lay it down in likelihood.
But if all aim but this be levell'd false,
The supposition of the lady's death
Will quench the wonder of her infamy.
And if it sort not well, you may conceal her,
As best befits her wounded reputation,
In some reclusive and religious life,
Out of all eyes, tongues, minds, and injuries.

There probably is no prettier example in all literature of a dramatist making fun of the ostensibly serious. The space between the Friar's ponderosity and tragic statement is very thin, but wide enough to encourage Shakespeare's demanded response, a chuckle, if not laughter. I rather despair of readers seeing this last joke. I have tried for three decades to explain it to stony-faced sophomores!

# 9

# Asymmetry in the First Scene of "Richard II"

$\mathcal{A}$sk any reader about the structure of Act 1, Scene 1 of *Richard II* and he will tell you that it is one of the most formally balanced scenes Shakespeare ever wrote. If he were told that Shakespeare deliberately employs asymmetry in it, he would, I am sure, disbelieve the assertion. He would be on good grounds, for Shakespeare here cleverly uses symmetry to create subtly the effect of asymmetry. Balance conceals imbalance, and it is through this geometric juggling that Shakespeare sets at once the character of the king whom this drama sets forth. A director who does not understand what Shakespeare is doing will omit an effect that is extremely important. The ways in which Richard moves and speaks should be dictated in a positive manner by the particular design or lack of design that Shakespeare is creating.

Alerted to the problem, reader and director, actor and spectator will understand the initial direction: "Enter King Richard, John of Gaunt with other nobles and attendants."

King Richard immediately queries Bolingbroke's father as to the charge that his son has made against Mowbray. The King's words "boisterous late appeal" applied to Bolingbroke should be disturbing, should indicate, since they are not followed by similar language for Mowbray, that Richard is not going to be impartial. Then enter Bolingbroke and Mowbray. Each addresses the King. Richard thanks each. Bolingbroke delivers a speech. Bolingbroke throws down his gage. Mowbray lifts it up. Again Richard indicates bias:

*King:*     What doth our cousin lay to Mowbray's charge?
    It must be great that can inherit us
    So much as of a thought of ill in him.

Bolingbroke makes his accusation. In the latter part of his speech there is a Biblical reference to Abel which cannot be understood except through the assumption that Mowbray in the matter of Gloucester's murder has been the agent of one of Gloucester's close relatives, who, therefore, was really responsible for the latter's murder:

> Which blood, like sacrificing Abel's, cries
> Even from the tongueless caverns of the earth
> To me for justice and rough chastisement;
> And, by the glorious worth of my descent,
> This arm shall do it, or this life be spent.

Again the King's words indicate bias against Bolingbroke, "How high a pitch his resolution soars!" Asking Mowbray for his reply, the King asserts, "Impartial are our eyes and ears." Mowbray then denies the charge. The King's ensuing speech lets the cat out of the bag and tends to express wholly and completely why we have felt some definite lack of proportion in the preceding formal balance of blocking and speech-making:

*King:*    Wrath-kindled gentlemen, be ruled by me;
    Let's purge this choler without letting blood.
    This we prescribe, though no physician;
    Deep malice makes too deep incision.
    Forget, forgive; conclude and be agreed;
    Our doctors say this is no month to bleed.
    Good uncle, let this end where it begun;
    We'll calm the Duke of Norfolk, you your son.

I am not pointing at the inappropriateness of the King's careless good humor before the solemnity of the occasion. I am pointing out that an imbalance which has been present from the start and felt rather than observed here becomes ostensible. The King is saying that he will act upon Mowbray as Gaunt is to act upon Bolingbroke. In other words the judge who was supposed to be the impartial listener and decider before the plaintiff-and-his-advocate and the defendant-and-his-advocate becomes the advocate of the defendant! If Richard is to be to the Duke of Norfolk as Gaunt is to be to his son, then the Abel reference earlier becomes clear: the source of our ill ease before apparent balance, but actual imbalance, becomes clear. Richard never has been impartial. The judge always has been the advocate. A group that should have always been five has always been four. The King should always have been a being separate from the litigants.

And a director should know this. Along with a subtle predisposition in manner to Mowbray and an enforcing of the particular speeches that I have called attention to, the actor who plays the King should also in his movements form and break the design of one before four: When he is the impartial King, there is a gap on Mowbray's side; when he is on Mowbray's side, there should be a gap in the judgeship. Thus by blocking, by personal inclination demonstrably breaking through the *persona,* by the use of hand and voice, Richard

141

should indicate that he is not impartial, that he is the confederate of Mowbray, and that Bolingbroke is resented and feared by him.

The rest of the scene is easy to understand from this viewpoint.

*Gaunt:*    To be a make-peace shall become my age.
  Throw down, my son, the Duke of Norfolk's gage.
*King:*    And, Norfolk, throw down his.
*Gaunt:*                    When, Harry? when?
  Obedience bids I should not bid again.
*King:*    Norfolk, throw down, we bid. There is no boot.
*Mowb:* Myself, I throw, dread sovereign, at thy foot.
  My life thou shalt command, but not my shame.
  The one my duty owes; but my fair name,
  Despite of death that lives upon my grave,
  To dark dishonour's use thou shalt not have.
  I am disgraced, impeached, and baffled here;
  Pierced to the soul with slander's venomed spear,
  The which no balm can cure but his heart-blood
  Which breathed this poison.

Note that Mowbray's reply is one addressed not only to his King but also to his advocate. Immediately however the King returns to his role of impartiality. First he turns to Mowbray, "Rage must be withstood./Give me his gage. Lions make leopards tame." Then he turns to Bolingbroke, "Cousin, throw up your gage. Do you begin."

The scene ends with the King's spineless declaration that although he was "not born to sue, but to command," their combat is to come upon St. Lambert's day at Coventry. But we feel already that the King cannot afford to let the match come off. And we are definitely also prepared for the revelation by Gaunt in the next scene that the judge is the murderer.

God's is the quarrel; for God's substitute,
His deputy anointed in his sight,
Hath caused his death; the which if wrongfully,
Let heaven revenge; for I may never lift
An angry arm against his minister.

And so consequential has the imbalance been—the judge being the accomplice—that we are prepared for the fracturing of God's design in the ensuing events, the usurpation by Bolingbroke of Richard's position.

143

# 10

## The Modern Othello

Is the Othello of modern critics Shakespeare's Othello?

Here are three representative opinions. To Sir Edmund Chambers, Othello is "the simple open-hearted soldier," "a gracious and doomed creature" who is an "easy victim."[1] For Kittredge, he is "an heroic and simple nature, putting full trust in two friends, both of whom betray him, the one in angry malice, the other by weakness and self-seeking."[2] Stoll sees him as a very noble dramatic puppet who evinces no psychological consistency in his passage from love to sudden jealousy and who must fall because of the dramatic devices that everyone trusts the villain: Iago is Othello's nemesis.[3]

I do not think that these Othellos are Shakespeare's Othello. I do not think that these are the Othello whom the judicious reader or spectator or actor sees. I do not think that these are the Othello whom an Elizabethan audience saw. Theodore Spencer is more cautious: "It is solely because Othello is the

**145**

kind of man that he is that a man like Iago can destroy him." [4] Yet what kind of man is the Moor? I think that Shakespeare gives the answer partially by means of contrast within the play.

Consider the following speech of Iago to Roderigo in 1.2, when the latter says that it is not in his power to control his love for Desdemona:

> . . . 'Tis in ourselves that we are thus or thus. Our bodies are our gardens, to the which our wills are gardeners; so that if we will plant nettles or sow lettuce, set hyssop and weed up thyme, supply it with one gender of herbs or distract it with many, either to have it sterile with idleness or manured with industry, why, the power and corrigible authority of this lies in our wills. If the balance of our lives had not one scale of reason to poise another of sensuality, the blood and baseness of our natures would conduct us to most preposterous conclusions; but we have reason to cool our raging motions, our carnal stings, our unbitted lusts, whereof I take this that you call love to be a sect or scion.

Shakespeare, says Kittredge, uses Iago "for the utterance of great truths. Of all these the most remarkable is his sublime assertion (to Roderigo) of the supremacy of will and reason in the cultivation of the moral faculties. . . . That is a saying of which Hamlet himself might be proud, and to which the noble Brutus would assent with enthusiasm." [5] Yet Iago's statement is simple Christian catechism. It is "the true doctrine" which is uttered by Jack Cade in the *Mirror for Magistrates*.[6] If this doctrine be noble, then the Othello of modern critics is not noble, for they assert that he is not the maker of his own destiny: Iago is. But if we are going to insist on understanding Elizabethan dramatic artifice, let us also insist on examining *Othello* according to the traditional values which

146

Shakespeare has injected implicitly and explicitly into the play. Actually by stressing Othello's innocence, modern critics have robbed the character of what the Elizabethans considered man's highest dignity—his own responsibility for his own life and character. Othello is less innocuous than modern critics conceive him because he ultimately *is* responsible for his terrible fate. On the other hand, precisely because of this responsibility, he possesses a stature as tragic protagonist which without this responsibility he could not possess.

Modern critics exonerate Othello. The noble hero is not responsible for the catastrophe. It is the devil-man, Iago, who is. But Othello is not the only noble character in the play who falls because of the wiles of Iago. Cassio does too. But Cassio does not excuse himself of culpability. He, too, follows the doctrine laid down by Iago above. Let us examine 2.3.268 ff. Knowing that he should not drink, Cassio has listened to the tempter, Iago, has become drunk in consequence, has created a scene, and has been dismissed from office:

*Cassio:* I will rather sue to be despis'd than to deceive so good a commander with so slight, so drunken, and so indiscreet an officer. Drunk? and speak parrot? and squabble? swagger? swear? and discourse fustian with one's own shadow? O thou invisible spirit of wine, if thou hast no name to be known by, let us call thee devil! . . . I remember a mass of things, but nothing distinctly; a quarrel, but nothing wherefore. O God, that men should put an enemy in their mouths to steal away their brains! That we should, with joy, pleasance, revel, and applause, transform ourselves into beasts!

*Iago:* Why, but you are now well enough. How come you thus recovered?

*Cassio:* It hath pleas'd the devil drunkenness to give place to the devil wrath. One unperfectness shows me another, to make me frankly despise myself.

147

*Iago:* Come, you are too severe a moraler. As the time, the place, and the condition of this country stands, I could heartily wish this had not befallen; but since it is as it is, mend it for your own good.

*Cassio:* I will ask him for my place again; he shall tell me I am a drunkard! Had I as many mouths as Hydra, such an answer would stop them all. To be now a sensible man, by and by a fool, and presently a beast! O strange! Every inordinate cup is unbless'd and the ingredient is a devil.

Clearly Cassio considers that his succumbing to the devil was his own fault. He does not exonerate himself of responsibility for his own ruin. An Elizabethan audience would not have understood a dramatist who implied that the Devil was invariably man's nemesis.

But, says Stoll constantly, the question of choice does not enter into the matter of Othello's believing Iago. It is a dramatic convention that Iago's mask is impenetrable. All the characters believe him to be honest. Hence, Othello *must* believe Iago's slander against Desdemona.

It is true that Shakespeare has artfully maintained the fiction of Iago's honesty among the *dramatis personae.* But Shakespeare is more artful than Stoll notes. There are three clean-cut occasions in the play when the characters do not believe Iago. And each of these occasions occurs when he suggests that Desdemona is unchaste! Or let us put the matter a different way. Iago tells four of the characters that Desdemona is unchaste—and the only one who believes this accusation is Othello! It may be stated categorically that, contrary to Stoll, Shakespeare has underlined the premise that Othello need not have believed Iago's imputations.

In 2.1, after the arrival scene in Cyprus, Iago asserts to Roderigo that Desdemona is in love with Cassio. "With him?

148

Why, 'tis not possible." Iago persists: Cassio is "a pestilent complete knave, and the woman hath found him already." But Roderigo answers, "I cannot believe that in her. She's full of most bless'd condition." And when Iago points to seeming proof, "Did'st thou not see her paddle with the palm of his hand? Did'st not mark that?" Roderigo refuses to believe him: "Yes, that I did; but that was but courtesy." The next scene but one (2.3) is the scene of Cassio's downfall. But though Iago can tempt Cassio to drink, he cannot tempt him to disbelief in Desdemona's chastity:

*Cassio:* Welcome, Iago; we must to the watch.
*Iago:* Not this hour, Lieutenant; 'tis not yet ten o' th' clock. Our general cast us thus early for the love of his Desdemona; who let us not therefore blame. He hath not yet made wanton the night with her; and she is sport for Jove.
*Cassio:* She's a most exquisite lady.
*Iago:* And, I'll warrant her, full of game.
*Cassio:* Indeed, she's a most fresh and delicate creature.
*Iago:* What an eye she has! Methinks it sounds a parley to provocation.
*Cassio:* An inviting eye; and yet methinks right modest.
*Iago:* And when she speaks, is it not an alarum to love?
*Cassio:* She is indeed perfection.
*Iago:* Well, happiness to their sheets! Come, Lieutenant, I have a stoup of wine; and here without are a brace of Cyprus gallants that would fain have a measure to the health of black Othello.

And the very denouement of the play depends on one character's having more faith in Desdemona than in Iago. When Emilia first hears that *her own husband* has said that Desdemona was unfaithful, she cries, "He lies to the heart" (5.2.159). Thus, by having Iago always believed except in the matter of Desdemona's morality and believed in this matter

149

only by Othello, Shakespeare is certainly using the dramatic device of contrast for a purpose. And what can this purpose be but to indicate that there is something in Othello's character which leads him to believe Iago's calumny concerning his wife?

But what is this something? T. S. Eliot has made an illuminating statement concerning Othello's final great speech, "Soft you; a word or two before you go," etc.

> What Othello seems to me to be doing in making this speech is *cheering himself up*. He is endeavouring to escape reality, he has ceased to think about Desdemona, and is thinking about himself. Humility is the most difficult of all virtues to achieve; nothing dies harder than the desire to think well of oneself. Othello succeeds in turning himself into a pathetic figure, but adopting an *aesthetic* rather than a moral attitude, dramatizing himself against his environment. He takes in the spectator, but the human motive is primarily to take in himself. I do not believe that any writer has ever exposed this *bovarysme*, the human will to see things as they are not, more clearly than Shakespeare.[7]

But Eliot could have gone much further. In this last scene there is much evidence that Othello refuses to look squarely at his crime. Fate was responsible: "But, O vain boast!/Who can control his fate? 'tis not so now" (267-8). Or it was the stars: "O ill-starr'd wench!" (275). Or his motive was of the best: He is "An honourable murderer. . . . /For nought I did in hate, but all in honour!" (297-8). Contrast this self-exculpation with the attitude of Cassio toward *his* fall which we discussed earlier. There is little doubt, I believe, that the Othello of the last scene is not quite so strong a character as critics have made him out to be.[8] He is understandably human, but he is not greatly noble.

It is this, the refusal to face reality, this, the trait of self-idealization, which makes of Shakespeare's Othello a psychologically consistent characterization and which explains why he falls so quickly into Iago's trap, why he alone on Iago's instigation believes Desdemona a strumpet.

Stoll maintains that Othello's belief in Iago is not grounded in Othello's psychology but is merely Shakespeare's dramatic device. "And it is only . . . by means of a specious and unreal psychology that he is made incapable of distrusting the testimony which his nature forbids him to accept, to the point of distrusting the testimony and character of those whom both his nature and their own forbid him to discredit." [9] Accordingly, Stoll belabors those critics who have attempted to see Othello as a psychologically consistent character.

It is interesting to see the way Stoll reasons. Again and again, when in discussing characters he says that Shakespeare substitutes artifice for authentic psychology, it is always Stoll's own concept of psychology which is the criterion. It may be, indeed, that the "psychology" of the critics whom Stoll attacks is entirely false. It does not follow that the "psychology" which Stoll employs to disprove them is correct. It is possible that Shakespeare's knowledge of how certain human beings operate in given situations is better than Stoll's. One is very much inclined to believe this merely on *a priori* grounds when he reads the following sentence in the midst of Stoll's rebuttal of those who have tried to read Othello's character: "Psychology, like law, is common sense, though art itself need not be." [10] No one who has any knowledge of the human heart and mind— whether he be a psychiatrist, or a psychologist, or a literary critic interested in determining to what extent art reflects life, or a spectator in the theater—will be inclined to agree with Stoll.

As a matter of fact, so irrational can human behavior be

151

that in order to create probability the dramatist has to make his characters more consistent than people are in real life. It is a measure of Shakespeare's greatness that his probable characters are also possible characters.[11] When Shakespeare created Othello, he was merely imitating a life that produces a Rousseau or a William Blake, romantic idealists who swing from overtrust to unjust suspicion in a twinkling. Emotional polarity is one of the commonest traits of humanity. We all have a touch of paranoia in us. To the extent that we acclaim our own greatness (i.e., escape reality), to that extent do we suspect others. This is not common sense—but it is life. And Shakespeare imitates life. And the spectator reacts to this imitation not with technical knowledge but with awareness of human nature.

Othello from the beginning is too much of a romantic idealist, in regard to himself and others. He considers human nature superior to what it actually is. He overvalues Desdemona as much as he overvalues Iago, and himself.[12] In 4.3, Emial discusses sex in blunt unromantic terms. And her husband tells Othello in 3.3.142-5:

> Who has that breast so pure
> But some uncleanly apprehensions
> Keep leets and law-days and in sessions sit
> With meditations lawful?

And even Desdemona in 3.4.149 says: "Nay, we must think men are not gods." But now listen to Othello when we see him and Desdemona together for the first time, when she has just pleaded to be allowed to go to Cyprus with him (1.3.260 ff.):[13]

*Othello:* Your voyces Lords: beseech you let her will
  Haue a free way, I therefore beg it not

152

To please the pallat of my appetite,
Nor to comply with heate, the young affects
In [me] defunct, and proper satisfaction,
But to be free and bounteous of her mind,
And heauen defend your good soules that you thinke
I will your serious and good businesse scant,
For she is with me;—no, when light-wing'd toyes,
And feather'd Cupid foyles with wanton dulnesse,
My speculatiue and actiue instruments,
That my disports, corrupt and taint my businesse,
Let huswiues make a skellet of my Helme,
And all indigne and base aduersities,
Make head against my reputation.

*Duke:* Be it, as you shall priuately determine,
Either for stay or going, the affaires cry hast,
And speede must answer, you must hence to night,

*Desdemona:* To night my Lord?

*Duke:* This night.

*Othello:* With all my heart.

Note how carefully Shakespeare distinguishes between Desdemona's cry (This is their wedding night!) and Othello's almost inhuman, "With all my heart."

Just as Othello flees from facing what he is in the last act, so too does he flee from what he is in the above speech in the first act.[14] That which makes him psychologically consistent is his refusal to see himself as ordinarily human.[15] The importance of 1.3.260-74, in which Othello disclaims sexual feelings, is that it furnishes the spectator with the first clear indication that Othello considers himself above human passions. From that time on the spectator will watch for repetition of this dangerous self-delusion and evidence that indicates it is a delusion. The spectator will contrast the Platonic exhilaration of the "O my fair warrior!" passage (2.1.180 ff.) with the sexuality of "Come, my dear love," etc. (2.3.8-10). The spectator will

153

be prepared for the outbreak of passion dissolving judgment in 3.3, by Othello's outburst toward the drunken Cassio in 2.3.196-9:

> Now, by heaven,
> My blood begins my safer guides to rule;
> And passion, having my best judgment collied,
> Assays to lead the way.

Here, for the first time, the god pose clearly dissolves. The spectator will observe self-delusion permeating the temptation scene (3.3) in which Othello disclaims attitudes and emotions which he immediately exhibits. The spectator will see Othello holding on to his high opinion of himself in 4.1.40: "Nature would not invest herself in such shadowing passion without some instruction. It is not words that shakes me thus." When Iago tells Othello that he must have patience or the former will consider him "all in all in spleen," the spectator will hear Othello say, "I will be found most cunning in my patience" (4.1.90) though word and act deny him. The spectator will see grating sensuality and the god pose held concomitantly in 5.2.13-22. The conjunction of "I'll smell it on the tree" and self-justification is pretty ghastly. I quote Kittredge's note in his individual edition on lines 21-22: *"This sorrow's heavenly . . . love"*: "My sorrow is like that which God feels when he punishes the guilty: he loves the sinner, yet punishes the sin. Cf. *Hebrews,* xii, 6: 'Whom the Lord loveth he chasteneth.' Here again we see that Othello regards himself as the agent of divine justice. He strives to maintain this attitude of mind throughout the scene, but in vain." In short, the spectator will not, like Stoll, accept Othello's description of himself as "one not easily jealous" in 5.2.348, as a trustworthy remark, for it comes from one who from the first has believed himself to be what actually he is not.

154

Othello's romantic idealism has made him overidealize himself and Desdemona from the first. And like other romantic idealists, his overtrust speedily shifts to undertrust on the first provocation. Careful readers of the temptation scene (3.3) will observe how Othello cooperates with Iago, how Iago seems rather to make Othello see what corruption is within himself than to put something there which has not been there.

> There is terrible truth in the reflection that if a man is wedded to his fantasy of woman as the steadfast hiding-place of his heart, the fountain whence his current flows, so that he grows frantic and blind with passion at the thought of the actual woman he has married as a creature of natural varying impulse—then he lies at the mercy of life's chances, and of his own secret fears and suspicions.[16]

Paradoxically, Othello loves Desdemona so much that it is questionable whether in human terms he loves her at all. He loves not Desdemona but *his image of her*. (Shelley was such another.) To Othello, his wife is not a woman but the matrix of his universe.[17] And to Othello he himself is not a man but a super-being without ordinary human emotions. I never read the Othello speech above without recalling Juliet's passionate hymeneal, "Gallop apace," etc. (3.2.1-31). Why does Iago say of Othello in relation to Desdemona (2.3.331-7):

> And then for her
> To win the Moor, were't to renounce his baptism,
> All seals and symbols of redeemed sin,
> His soul is so enfettr'd to her love,
> That she may make, unmake, do what she list,
> Even as her appetite shall play the god
> With his weak function.

Othello, Iago is indicating here, keeps no proportion in his love. And there is no proportion in his fall. What makes of him a consistent character is a species of romantic idealism which soars, shatters, and partially recovers—which at no time, Shakespeare indicates by contrast, is ever to be taken on its own terms as modern critics tend to take it—which at no time, one can say, is completely equivalent with a nobility based on what the world is and not on what it is not.

Concerning this view, however, critics may say that I avoid the crucial descriptions of Othello by Iago:

> The Moor is of a free and open nature,
> That thinks men honest that but seem to be so,
> And will as tenderly be led by th' nose
> As asses are (1.3.393-6).

> The Moor, howbeit that I endure him not,
> Is of a constant, loving, noble nature,
> And I dare think he'll prove to Desdemona
> A most dear husband. (2.1.282-5)

Of course both these statements are choral. The first supports my analysis. It is a cynically realistic judgment of Othello's particular kind of nobility. What better definition of a romantic idealist can we find than that he is one "That thinks men honest that but seem to be so"—including himself? And the second statement is followed by lines which indicate that Othello can be made jealous "even to madness." There is no difficulty here in reconciling how Iago sees Othello and how the spectator sees him. The trouble is that critics tend to see him as he sees himself. Do we take other self-deluded characters on their own terms—Angelo, Romeo, Lear, Timon, Hotspur?

For Othello is not the only self-deluded character in Shakespeare's plays who thinks himself more ideal than actuality permits. Consider Romeo in his relationship with Rosaline.[18] Remember what happens to Angelo in *Measure for Measure.* Of him, at the opening of the play, the Duke says (1.3.50-4):

156

> Lord Angelo is precise,
> Stands at guard with envy, scarce confesses
> That his blood flows, or that his appetite
> Is more to bread than stone; hence shall we see,
> If power change purpose, what our seemers be.

There is probably more likeness between Othello and Angelo than critics care to find.[19] Doesn't Othello fail in the test too? And there is one other Shakespeare character who suddenly swings from the high pinnacle of an idealism which is not based on reality to a ghastly misanthropy, which, also, is not based on reality. Of Timon of Athens, Apemantus says, "The middle of humanity thou never knewest, but the extremity of both ends" (4.3.300-1). How apt these words are for Othello, too! That an outwardly noble character could fall because of an inner flaw, Shakespeare had indicated by means of Proteus even in the early *The Two Gentlemen of Verona*. And what of the thrice-noble Macbeth?

In short, it seems to me that by means of Iago's soliloquies; by means of character contrast with the brutally clear-eyed Iago, the earthy Emilia, the self-honest Cassio (who, also, be it remembered, openly admits his relationship to Bianca); by means of action contrast in the rejoinders of Roderigo, Cassio, and Emilia to the proposal that Desdemona is unchaste; by means of Othello's own words in the first and second acts; by means of a carefully drawn Othello in the temptation scene who considers himself much stronger than he actually is; by means of sundry touches throughout which show Othello refusing to recognize his own passionate nature; by means of a broken Othello in the last act, who tries to hang on to his nobility by refusing to face the fact of his murder—by means of all this Shakespeare has shown us that his hero is not as strong or as good a man as he thinks he is, that the hero's flaw is his refusal to face the reality of his own nature. This Othello, who (I think) is the Othello Shakespeare intended to convey, is rather different from the modern Othello, who is always thoroughly noble—before, during, and after his downfall. The truly noble aspects of Othello I have not stressed. They are obvious. The blots on the scutcheon I have stressed, for critics have obscured them.

The Othello that Shakespeare presents is nobly tragic in the same sense in which Macbeth and Antony and Coriolanus and Lear are nobly tragic. Shakespeare's tragic protagonist is noble, but he is not altogether noble. He represents Aristotle's dictum:

> A man not preeminently virtuous and just, whose misfortune, however, is brought upon him not by vice or depravity but by some error of judgment, he being one of those who enjoy great reputation and prosperity. . . . The change in the hero's fortunes must be . . . from happiness to misery; and the cause of it must lie not in any depravity, but in some great error on his part; the man himself being either such as we have described, or better, not worse, than that. (*Poetics,* Chapter 13)

It is not the hero's nobility in Shakespeare's tragedies but the flaw, the sin or error that all flesh is heir to, that destroys him. It is the close interweaving of great man, mere man, and base man that makes of Othello the peculiarly powerful and mysterious figure he is. In him Shakespeare shows the possible greatness, the possible baseness not only closely allied in what is after all mere man but also so causally connected that one must perforce wonder and weep.[20]

*Notes*

## NOTE TO ESSAY 1.

1. I am not the only critic who sees Shylock as evocative of the dislike of the Puritans. See E. E. Stoll, "Shakespeare's Jew," in *From Shakespeare to Joyce* (Garden City, 1944), pp. 126, 134, and Paul N. Siegle, "Shylock and the Puritan Usurers," in *Studies in Shakespeare* (Miami, Fla., 1953), pp. 129-38.

## NOTES TO ESSAY 3.

1. *Cf.* Kenneth Muir, Arden ed., 1951, p. lxvi.
2. The poetic design in which Edgar is here involved is complex. Before Poor Tom enters, the Fool sees the king who has given away his authority and possessions as a houseless beggar. "Fortune, that arrant whore,/Ne'er turns the key to the poor" (2.4.51-2). "The man that makes his toe/What he his heart should make," *i.e.,* Lear, is equivalent to the houseless beggar of the preceding four lines (3.2.27-32). Gloucester's lessoning runs parallel to Lear's. Blinded, he remembers Poor Tom, "Which made me think a man a worm" (4.1.34). And he gives Poor Tom his purse; "Let the superfluous and lust-dieted man" who "will not see/Because he does not feel" be punished by heaven so that he learns to "feel" (4.1.68-70).

## NOTES TO ESSAY 4.

1. *Shakespearean Tragedy* (London, 1937), pp. 152-53.
2. Q2: "Florish. Enter Claudius, King of Denmarke, Gertrad the Queene,

Counsaille: as Polonius, and his Sonne Laertes, Hamlet, Cum Alijs." F: "Enter Claudius King of Denmarke, Gertrude the Queene, Hamlet, Polonius, Laertes, and his Sister Ophelia, Lords Attendant."

3. Both Polonius and Laertes use the word *fashion* for Hamlet's attentions to Ophelia: "a fashion, and a toy in blood"; "Ay, fashion you may call it." As a matter of fact, it seems to be a family word; Ophelia uses it too for Hamlet: "importun'd me with love/In honourable fashion."

4. Compare Hamlet's sterner morality in 3.3. He will kill Claudius when the latter is not in a state of grace, when he is drunk, angry, in incestuous pleasure, "At gaming, swearing, or about some act/That hath no relish of salvation in't."

5. Johnson deplores his "useless and wanton cruelty" to "Ophelia, the young, the beautiful, the harmless, and the pious" and his savagery to the praying Claudius.—*Johnson's Shakespeare* (1765), VIII, 311, 236. Steevens points out the "immoral tendency" of Hamlet's character, the not "very warrantable means" by which he "pursued his ends" and agrees with Akenside that "the conduct of Hamlet was every way unnatural and indefensible."—*Steeven's Shakespeare* (1778), X, 412-13. G. Wilson Knight, *The Wheel of Fire* (rev. ed., London, 1949), pp. 17-46, 298-325; *The Imperial Theme* (London, 1931), pp. 96-124. L. C. Knights, *Explorations* (New York, 1947), pp. 82-93.

6. Harold Goddard, "In Ophelia's Closet," *Yale Review,* XXXV (1945), 462-474.

7. *The Wheel of Fire,* p. 21.

8. *Shakespere and His Predecessors* (New York, 1896), p. 398.

9. *Shakespearean Tragedy,* pp. 155-56.

10. *Prefaces to Shakespeare* (Princeton, 1946), I, 68.

11. Robert Bridges, "The Influence of the Audience on Shakespeare's Drama," in *Collected Essays Papers &c.* (Oxford), I (1927), 27: "Again, why are we forbidden to know anything concerning his earlier relations with Ophelia, how long he loved her, and how deeply? *Why is even the date of that strange letter hopelessly obscured,* unless it were that any one definite determination of it would expose or create a contradiction?" (Italics mine.)

12. Compare Hamlet's deliberately bad impromptu poetry: "For thou dost know, O Damon dear" and "For if the King like not the comedy" in 3.2 and "Imperious Caesar, dead and turn'd to clay" in 5.1.

13. *Some Remarks on the Tragedy of Hamlet* (London, 1736), quoted in C. C. H. Williamson, ed., *Readings on the Character of Hamlet, 1661-1947* (London, 1950), p. 7.

14. Salvador De Madariaga, *On Hamlet* (London, 1948), pp. 39-40: "Now is this a love letter at all? There are eminent authorities—Dowden one

160

of them—who say it is. No girl of average feminine acumen would take such stuff for the style of love. 'To the celestial, and my soul's idol, the most beautified Ophelia' might do for Osric; but from Hamlet's pen it can only mean *fun*. He is having fun out of her as he does out of everybody; playing *on* her as if she were an instrument. The mood is the same as that of his talk to, or rather, through, Osric. 'Most beautified Ophelia' does mean 'most made-up Ophelia'; not merely because it tallies with 'I have heard of your paintings' at 3.1, but (which is even more to the point) because Hamlet was not a man who could write *beautified* when he meant *beautiful;* so that the argument that 'Polonius' condemnation of *beautified* is sufficient to show that it is an innocent word' should be inverted: it shows that Hamlet did not mean it in the sense in which Polonius rightly criticised it. Then come four lines of doggerel which Hamlet must have known had nothing to do with either genuine love or genuine poetry:

> Doubt thou the stars are fire
> Doubt that the sun doth move,
> Doubt truth to be a liar
> But never doubt I love.

and then the 'O bother' perfunctory paragraph: 'O dear Ophelia, I am ill at these numbers, I have not art to reckon my groans, but that I love thee best, O most best, believe it. Adieu. Thine evermore, most dear lady, whilst this machine is to him, Hamlet.'—If that is the way Shakespeare made Hamlet express his love for Ophelia, he who has endowed the English language with one of the richest anthologies of love the world possesses, from the adolescent love of Romeo to the autumnal and hectic love of Anthony, we are right in concluding that Hamlet was at no time in love with Ophelia."

15. Granville-Barker, *Prefaces to Shakespeare,* I, 165.
16. Cambridge, Mass. (1945), pp. 152-55.
17. Edith Sitwell, *A Notebook on William Shakespeare* (London, 1948), p. 86.
18. *Shakespeare: A Survey* (London, 1935), p. 196.
19. It is at last in the play-scene that Granville-Barker sees Hamlet as cruel to Ophelia. "He sees her now as the demure decoy, the hypocrite, the wanton at heart; and on her, at least, he can be swiftly and cruelly revenged. It is the first outcropping of his cruelty, that flaw in a nature sensitive even to weakness, ever tempted to shirk its battle against the strong to triumph over one weaker still" (*Prefaces to Shakespeare,* I, 85). But this tends to omit one of the refinements of Hamlet's cruelty, calculation. As to "first outcropping," if cruelty be defined as making other

people uncomfortable, Hamlet was cruel from his very first appearance in 1.2.

20. Bridges, *op. cit.,* pp. 25-26.

## NOTES TO ESSAY 5.

1. *Character Problems in Shakespeare's Plays* (New York, 1922), p. 132.

2. *Ibid.,* pp. 121-27.

3. *Ibid.,* pp. 128, 138, *passim.*

4. *A Sketch of Recent Shakespearean Investigation,* 1893-1923 (London, 1923), pp. 49-50.

5. *Shakespeare Studies* (New York, 1927), p. 144, footnote 40.

6. I employ the text of the *7th* Arden edition, ed. R. H. Case, London, 1934.

7. Because of this double fear, Cleopatra refuses to descend from the monument at the dying Antony's request but has him drawn up instead (4.15.21-9). After she is taken prisoner, she vehemently tells Proculeius that "This mortal house I'll ruin" before she will be showed to "the shouting varletry/Of censuring Rome" or chastened by "the sober eye/Of dull Octavia" (5.2.49-62). She asks Dolabella whether Caesar intends to lead her in triumph, and he replies in the affirmative (106-10). He tells her this again, and adds, "Make your best use of this," and she thanks him greatly (197-206). She then in disgust tells Iras what will happen to them in Rome (206-20). Self-inflicted death is "the way/To fool their preparation" (223-5). Even before Cleopatra herself reveals this double fear, Antony taunts her with "Caesar's triumph" and "patient Octavia" in 4.12.32-9. Caesar, too, guesses the power of this fear when he sends Proculeius to her "Lest, in her greatness, by some mortal stroke/ She do defeat us" and rob him of "in Rome/ . . . our triumph" (5.1.64-6).

8. *Character Problems,* p. 129.

9. (Oxford, 1931), pp. 290-322.

10. Caroline Spurgeon, *Shakespeare's Imagery and What It Tells Us* (New York, 1936), p. 377: "Other interesting functions of the images which I may just note here are . . . their aid to the revelation of the temperament and character of the person using them. This is most interesting, and might well be developed further."

11. There is still much to be done on the symbolism in *A & C.* By "much" I do not mean anything as ample as what Knight does or anything as limited as what Spurgeon does (*op. cit.,* pp. 349-54). She sees one motif; she does not see the counter-motif; Knight sees almost everything but employs not enough balance and discrimination. The play is literally drenched in direct and indirect references to eating and drinking. Yet Spurgeon in Chart VI indicates only twelve food *images* in *A & C!* In

this kind of interpretation, certainly attention to metaphor should not be divorced from attention to non-metaphor if both apply to the same object of activity. Knight appears to recognize this. In *A & C*, for example, Cleopatra's being compared to a feast, Antony's constant references (especially in Acts 3, 4) to feasting, and the feasting scene on Pompey's galley are all parts of Shakespeare's designment. The sword and snake references in the play are also important. The best, simplest, and most modest defence of this particular approach to Shakespeare's plays is to be found in Msgr. F. C. Kolbe, *Shakespeare's Way* (London, 1930), pp. vii-xii, 1-2. Msgr. Kolbe does not confine himself to iterative imagery. He is concerned with "deliberate repetition throughout the play of at least one set of words or ideas in harmony with the plot" (p. 2).

12. *Character Problems*, p. 122.

13. The sexual signification of "die" in the seventeenth century is made quite clear in Dryden's song in *Marriage a la Mode*, "Whilst Alexis lay press'd."—*The Poetical Works of John Dryden*, Student's Cambridge Edition, G. R. Noyes, ed. (Boston, 1909), p. 68; it is indicated too in Pandarus' song in *Troilus and Cressida*, 3.1.108; see also the last three lines of Isabella's speech in "The Insatiate Countess" in H. Harvey Wood, ed., *The Plays of John Marston* (Edinburgh and London, 1939), III, 114-6, 27; and the third stanza of Donne's *The Canonization*. It is unfortunate that this meaning has been excluded from *O.E.D.* The equivocal meaning of "nothing" may be understood from *Hamlet*, 3.2.114-6. For "celerity," cf., "O, let him [Alexas] marry a woman that cannot go" (1.2.60-1). Case's note to this last indicates that commentators have missed the point of Charmian's sentence completely. "Go" and "do" also had equivocal meanings: see Dryden's song and cf. 1.5.22, quoted above. Enobarbus' speech is packed with sexual puns. I discover, after writing the above lines, that Allen Tate discusses the double meaning of "die" in Donne's *Valediction Forbidding Mourning* on p. 91 of *Reason in Madness* (New York, 1941).

14. So does Antony, 4.14.99-101:

> But I will be
> A bridegroom in my death, and run into 't
> As to a lover's bed.

15. This speech inevitably recalls Enobarbus' "The barge she sat in," etc. (2.2.195-230).

16. This conception of her dead lover's getting up from where he is lying (in Elysian fields) and coming to meet her (281-5) recalls Antony's 4.14.50-4:

163

> Eros!—I come, my queen:—Eros!—Stay for me:
> Where souls do couch on flowers, we'll hand in hand,
> And with our sprightly port make the ghosts gaze:
> Dido and her Aeneas shall want troops,
> And all the haunt be ours.

Thus the voluptuary, Antony, conceives of death as does his mistress. See note 14. In Cleopatra's last words death and her lover seem to equate. Shakespeare seems to make Antony and Cleopatra deliberately echo each other in the last two acts. There is great significance in this, but the matter is too large to go into here.

17. Recall 1.5.27-8:

> Think on me,
> That am with Phoebus' amorous pinches black. . . .

The sexuality of lines 293-4 in Cleopatra's address to the dead Iras is obvious, but that of 291-2 is not. The image is one of two lovers parting after a kiss. In 293 death is the male lover; in 292 nature. I feel sure, too, that the imagery in 291-2 is that of two lovers parting after the climax of physical love.

18. Note how she conceives of the meeting with Antony after death as a lovers' assignation. Case's note on "curled" is instructive: "Probably she thinks of Antony as she first saw him, 'barber'd ten times o'er,' . . . again set off to the best advantage for this meeting, as she herself will be . . . in 'her best attires,' 'again for Cydnus,/To meet Mark Antony.' "

19. Shortly before (5.2.7-8), Cleopatra refers to death as a sleep in which one no longer requires the repulsive wet-nursing which "the dung" (i.e., the earth's food) provides for all. Hence, putting both passages together, we get: Life is disagreeable wet-nursing; Death is pleasant wet-nursing. Cf. Antony's 1.1.35-6: "Our dungy earth alike/Feeds beast as man."

20. Recall her 1.5.26-7: "now I feed myself/With most delicious poison."

## NOTES TO ESSAY 7.

1. In the last scene of the play, Hamlet, in listing Claudius' crimes against him, asserts that the latter "Popp'd in between the election and my hopes" (5.2.65). This is the first out-and-out declaration by the Prince that he had been ambitious for the kingship. That Rosencrantz states Hamlet thinks Denmark a prison because "your ambition makes it one" (2.2.252) is merely fishing: it tells us nothing of Hamlet's real thoughts.

2. The Duke says to Mariana (4.1.70-71):

> He is your husband an a pre-contract;
> To bring you thus together, 'tis no sin.

Claudio declares (1.2.138-42):

> upon a true contract
> I got possession of Julietta's bed.
> You know the lady, she is fast my wife,
> Save that we do the denunciation look
> Of outward order.

Unlike some critics, I cannot see the great distinction between the Angelo-Mariana "pre-contract" and the Claudio-Juliet "true contract." There is no more evidence for the *formality* of the former contract in the Duke's description to Isabella than for the latter contract. Furthermore I suspect that "denunciation . . . of outward order" does not refer to public announcement of betrothal but to marriage itself.

## NOTES TO ESSAY 10.

1. *Shakespeare: A Survey* (London, 1935), pp. 219, 225.
2. *Shakespeare* (Cambridge, Mass., 1930), p. 35.
3. *Art and Artifice in Shakespeare* (Cambridge, 1933), pp. 6-55, 173-4, *passim; Shakespeare and Other Masters* (Cambridge, Mass., 1940), pp. 59-84, *passim;* "Source and Motive in *Macbeth* and *Othello,*" *Review of English Studies,* 19 (1943), 25-32. The opinions of Stoll, Chambers, and Kittredge have been arbitrarily selected. Further examples of the same view can easily be found. For example, Dover Wilson says that "Iago's victim is blameless."—*The Essential Shakespeare* (New York and Cambridge, 1932), p. 120. For a most interesting consideration of Othello, far different from most, one which takes the Moor as a not totally assimilated black barbarian, see Mark Van Doren's *Shakespeare* (New York, 1939), pp. 225-37. To Van Doren, Othello "deserves his tragedy."
4. *Shakespeare and the Nature of Man* (New York, 1942), p. 124.
5. *Shakespeare,* pp. 45-6.
6. E. M. Tillyard, *The Elizabethan World Picture* (London, 1943), pp. 53-4.
7. "Shakespeare and the Stoicism of Seneca," in *Selected Essays: 1917-1932* (London, 1932), pp. 130-1. Stoll takes issue with this in *Art and Artifice in Shakespeare,* pp. 173-4. "As I have shown elsewhere this is a self-descriptive method . . . : if taken as a bit of self-consciousness, it much troubles the noble and heroic impression." The answer to this is, simply, that apparently Shakespeare did want this impression to be troubled. One cannot possibly take Othello on his own terms. Every single thing that

he says about himself in 3.3.181 ff., "Think'st thou I'ld make a life of jealousy," etc., is immediately disproved by the way he acts in the lines immediately succeeding.

Although Stoll constantly rebukes other critics for their "psychology," in answering Eliot he does not hesitate to invent his own "psychology": "And even as dramatic psychology—that is, such as does not press and peer behind drama and poetry—the speech is finely appropriate. After such an experience and such depths of despair Othello must, in sheer reaction and relapse, think a little well of himself. It is one of the glories of Shakespeare that . . . he recognizes the limits of human nature. . . ."

Then does Stoll agree with Eliot? The issue seems to be that the former sees the hero as thoroughly noble, the latter as imperfectly noble. However, Eliot also indicates the tension between these two viewpoints going on at one and the same time in the spectator, for Eliot himself is a spectator.

8. The final Othello is not a pretty sight to watch. Consider his whimpering (246-7 and 272-4), his refusal to be by himself (260-1), his uncontrolled screaming (280-5). I cannot see how Schücking can write of Othello that "Shakespeare's intention . . . was to create a hero who, for all his weakness in the matter of jealousy, never falls so low as to lose his dignity." —"The Baroque Character of the Elizabethan Tragic Hero," *Annual Shakespeare Lecture of the British Academy* (Oxford, 1938), p. 27. Critics state—but do no more than state—that Othello at the end is a better man than he has been before.—See A. C. Bradley, *Shakespearean Tragedy* (London and New York, 1906), p. 198; R. W. Chambers, *Man's Unconquerable Mind* (London and Toronto, 1939), pp. 261, 303; E. M. W. Tillyard, *Shakespeare's Last Plays* (London, 1938), pp. 17, 21. G. Wilson Knight, "The Othello Music," in *The Wheel of Fire* (Oxford, 1930), p. 130, does not claim growth but does claim that during the last scene "Othello is a nobly tragic figure."

9. *Othello* (Minneapolis, 1915), p. 33; quoted with a few changes in *Art and Artifice in Shakespeare,* p. 16.

10. *Art and Artifice in Shakespeare,* p. 17.

11. My underlying premise is that expressed by W. W. Lawrence, "Artifice must always be sustained by a due proportion of nature, of psychological consistency."—"Hamlet's Sea Voyage," *PMLA,* LIX (1944), 69.

12. See Maud Bodkin, *Archetypal Patterns in Poetry* (Oxford, 1934), pp. 217-24, 245, 332-4. This is probably the best psychological discussion of *Othello* to be found. But Miss Bodkin is interested in much broader matters than I am.

13. I quote from Quarto 1. because Folio omits Desdemona's question and the Duke's reply in 278. Modern texts differ, some following Q, some F.

166

14. Of this speech, Theodore Spencer (*Shakespeare and the Nature of Man,* pp. 127-8) writes: "His love for Desdemona is in keeping with such a character; entirely unlike the love of Troilus for Cressida, it has no sensuality in it. When he asks to be allowed to take Desdemona to Cyprus with him, he explicitly describes—in the terms of Elizabethan psychology —the exalted quality of his devotion: [Spencer quotes the speech.] Like Horatio, Othello appears to all the world as a man who is not passion's slave. His higher faculties, his 'speculative and offic'd instruments,' are apparently in complete control."

Is Othello, then, displaying sensuality when in Cyprus, in 2.3.8-10, he says to Desdemona:

> Come, my dear love.
> The purchase made, the fruits are to ensue;
> That profit's yet to come 'tween me and you.

Is Desdemona displaying "sensuality" when she cries, "Tonight, my lord?" Othello may play the noble stoic concerning marriage in 1.3. But he talks like a normal man concerning marriage in 2.3. And unless Shakespeare was extraordinarily careless, the two speeches were meant to contrast. In the first, Othello indicates that he is above men; in the second, that he is a man. He is a good man in the second, an extraordinary man (if honest) in the first. But since the second contradicts the first, Othello is neither extraordinary nor honest. Certainly an audience *feels* if it does not see something wrong in the first. One function of Iago's filth in 1.1 is certainly to indicate to the audience the sexual aspect of marriage.

15. Compare Othello's opinion of himself with Henry the Fifth's (*HV,* 4.1 100 ff.):

> For, though I speak it to you, I think the King is but a man, as I am. The violet smells to him as it does to me; the element shows to him as it doth to me; all his senses have but human conditions. His ceremonies laid by, in his nakedness he appears but a man; and though his affections are higher mounted than ours, yet, when they stoop, they stoop with the like wing.

16. Bodkin, *Archetypal Patterns,* p. 222.

17. "My life upon her faith" (1.3.294). "Excellent wretch! Perdition catch my soul, etc." (3.3.91-3). "If she be false, O, then heaven mocks itself!" (3.3.282). "O, now for ever/Farewell the tranquil mind!" etc. (3.3.351-61). The most notable expression of the total dependence of Othello on his image of Desdemona is in 4.2.48-65. "Had it pleas'd heaven," etc. But

these are explicit statements. His whole bearing toward Desdemona, especially in 2.1, the arrival in Cyprus scene, implies this view of her.

18. Objective analysis of this relationship is supplied by Friar Laurence in 2.3.64-82.

19. With Othello's denial and Iago's admission of human frailty cited above, cf. Isabella to Angelo (2.2.136-41):

> Go to your bosom;
> Knock there, and ask your heart what it doth know
> That's like my brother's fault. If it confess
> A natural guiltiness such as is his,
> Let it not sound a thought upon your tongue
> Against my brother's life.

20. Since writing the above, I have read an important little book, Allardyce Nicoll's *Studies in Shakespeare* (Hogarth Lectures No. 3, London, 1931). Since students of Shakespeare tend to distrust—and rightly—any character interpretation that differs sharply from the traditional view, I am happy to record that Professor Nicoll (though he uses a different approach, less inductive and comparative than impressionistic) has come to the same conclusion as I have—that Othello is a self-deceiving romantic idealist. Though he merely outlines rather than details (as I attempt), yet our interpretations even to the use sometimes of the same passages coincide remarkably. But I do not think that Professor Nicoll sees Othello as in tension between conflicting inward forces: he tends to strip him bluntly of *all* nobility.

*The manuscript was edited by Alexander Brede. The text type face is Linotype Granjon, designed in 1924 by George W. Jones, based on a face originally cut by Claude Garamond in the 16th Century. The display face is Bank Script from American Type Founders.*

*This book was printed on Warren's 1854 Text regular finish paper. The soft cover edition of this book was bound in Warren's Cameo Brilliant Cover and the hard cover edition was bound in Joanna Mills Natullin. This book was manufactured in the United States of America.*